Powerful & Free

CONFRONTING THE GLASS CEILING
FOR WOMEN
IN THE CHURCH

DANNY SILK

To Sheri

"Virtually every woman I know who has heard Danny Silk's message on *Powerful and Free* has found it to be literally life-changing. Rarely does one book have so much impact on so many women. It is a message the whole Church—no, the whole world—needs to hear!"

Stacey Campbell
WWW.NEWLIFE.BC.CA
WWW.BEAHERO.ORG

"We are crossing the gender gap in our generation. It's a one-way crossing with no return. Western culture crossed this bridge ahead of the Church—and ended up on an island in the midst of the raging sea of the most powerful enemy of womankind: radical feminism. It happened because the Church could not step up in response to the existential cry of woman who is made in the image of God. In *Powerful and Free: Confronting the Glass Ceiling for Women in the Church*, Danny steps up. His candid, personal journey takes us beneath the surface right to the heart of liberty and identity. This is a book for men, and every woman they love, for women and the men they admire. It's for fathers' daughters and for daughters' fathers, for disciples and their mentors, for married and single. We will not carry the carpetbag of ancient prejudice over to a new generation. If we have a ceiling, it will be a true and pure foundation for the coming ones to stand on and reach for the stars. With the Holy Spirit gingerly leading the way, *Powerful and Free* guides us from mutiny to mutuality and on toward the 'indispensible partnership in fulfilling God's commission to fill and subdue the earth.'"

Bonnie Chavda
CO-FOUNDER AND CO-PASTOR ALL NATIONS CHURCH &
THE WATCH OF THE LORD

"Danny's perspective on relational dynamics always inspires and...well, unnerves me. He paints a picture of the sort of person I want to be. One who doesn't just show up but arrives with gracious strength and a plan for how we can mutually thrive. As for unnerving, he has an uncanny ability to be in my head and dig out the hidden, self-serving spots in my worldview that I prefer not to see.

I especially appreciate his section on interpreting the key Biblical passages. Christians believe the Bible is authoritative in faith and practice, so we don't want to simply dismiss or ignore passages that contradict our viewpoint. Danny hasn't done this. Rather than 'explaining away' problematic passages, he 'explains them into' a proper context for interpretation and application and provides a solid Biblical foundation as we all experience transforming relationships that are powerful and free."

Dann Farrelly
ASSOCIATE PASTOR AT BETHEL CHURCH
DEAN OF BETHEL SCHOOL OF SUPERNATURAL MINISTRY

"Danny Silk has caught the heart of God in wanting His daughters to be *Powerful and Free*. As men, many of us have not fulfilled our role in ushering women into their assigned place of empowerment. Poor traditions and inconsistent biblical interpretation have fed into this problem. My home would not have the strength it has without my wife's strong influence. In the same way, we simply are not complete as a Church culture without empowered women taking their rightful place. This book will provoke you to think and take a renewed look at women's roles. Many men will be relieved to find biblical thought that supports their role in bringing women into their call and destiny. And women who read this book will find great joy as they recognize that God's heart is for them to have a significant contribution into what God is doing in the earth today."

Bill Johnson
SENIOR LEADER, BETHEL CHURCH
AUTHOR OF *WHEN HEAVEN INVADES EARTH* AND *HOSTING HIS PRESENCE*

"It is a great honor to endorse *Powerful and Free*. I've watched firsthand as Danny has championed women—creating a healthy culture, a safe place, and releasing them to be all that they want and can be. Danny tears down the walls that have held women and opens the door to understanding."

Beni Johnson
SENIOR LEADER, BETHEL CHURCH
AUTHOR OF *THE HAPPY INTERCESSOR*

"If you like shooting sacred cows so they never rise again, then Powerful and Free by Danny Silk is definitely for you. This book will both greatly encourage and challenge those who read it. It is honest and vulnerable, and I am confident that many who digest its contents will be set free to soar in their gifts and callings without restraint. Thank you, Danny, for this wonderful blessing."

Patricia King
WWW.XPMEDIA.COM
WWW.XPMINISTRIES.COM
WWW.PATRICIAKINGLIFECOACH.COM

"This is the book I have been waiting for! In his book, Powerful and Free, Danny Silk lifts the veil to reveal a reality for many women in the Church. I really believe this book is a catalyst to bring a new movement of freedom to the Body of Christ. I am thrilled to give my endorsement and look forward to witnessing the testimonies of lives changed!"

Kim Walker-Smith
JESUS CULTURE

"The topic of empowering women toward their full biblical portion and godly potential has been a passion in Danny's heart and a fire in his gut for years. Pentecostal denominations have ordained and commissioned women since their founding. Prior to that James Hudson Taylor employed single women in the evangelization of China. Neither thought such to be leftist, revisionist, or compromising, and the fruit has been good. Taking the gospel of Jesus Christ to the world is an all-hands project that requires women to be co-equal co-laborers in the Body of Christ. Danny's eyes are set on that mission."

Andre Van Mol, MD
BOARD-CERTIFIED FAMILY PHYSICIAN
BETHEL REDDING ELDER
BOARD MEMBER OF MORAL REVOLUTION ("ASK THE DOC" BLOGGER),
AND PRAYNORTHSTATE

"In 539 B.C., a Persian King named Ahasuerus threw his wife out of the palace and held a contest to find a new queen. A Jewish man named Mordecai emerged on the scene and convinced his beautiful cousin, Esther, to enter the contest; of course, she wins. All is well in the palace until a wicked villain named Haman convinced the King to annihilate all the Jews living in Persia. Mordecai re-emerged in Esther's life and desperately pleaded with Esther to use her favor to foil Haman's plot, and deliver her people from complete destruction. Esther courageously entered the King's chambers and ultimately rescues the Jews from extermination. Esther has rightfully become a legend, yet without Mordecai's admonishment she would have been just another pretty face and the Jews would be extinct.

Danny Silk's book, *Powerful and Free*, is not just another manuscript about women in leadership; it's a Mordecai Mandate, admonishing King's daughters everywhere to take their rightful place as co-heirs of the throne of grace. Through several life examples, Danny inspires men to shake off the shackles of religion and stand against the spirit of oppression by empowering women to co-lead with them.

One of the most compelling things about *Powerful and Free* is Danny's personal journey with his own wife, Sheri. His candid, honest, and transparent testimony about their painful marriage and their path to wholeness will capture your soul. Their agonizing relationship created a platform for Danny to learn how to free a powerful woman to thrive and succeed. This book is a 'must read' for every Christian man and woman. But PROCEED WITH CAUTION, as this book is a weapon of mass-destruction against the ancient, evil castles that have been erected in the minds of many to imprison half the population of the world!"

Kris Vallotton
SENIOR ASSOCIATE LEADER, BETHEL CHURCH
CO-FOUNDER OF BETHEL SCHOOL OF SUPERNATURAL MINISTRY
AUTHOR OF NINE BOOKS INCLUDING *THE SUPERNATURAL WAYS OF ROYALTY* AND *SPIRIT WARS*.

"I thought, *Here we go, another guy writing about women's role in the Church.* I was quite pleasantly surprised and impressed with Danny's perspective on and heart for the subject. Even I gleaned an important new perspective. It is a brilliant book and a must-read for both men and women! His perspective is very fresh and life-giving."

Barbara J. Yoder
SENIOR PASTOR AND LEAD APOSTLE
SHEKINAH REGIONAL EQUIPPING/REVIVAL CENTER
BREAKTHROUGH APOSTOLIC MINISTRIES NETWORK
WWW.SHEKINAHCHURCH.ORG
WWW.BARBARAYODERBLOG.COM

POWERFUL AND FREE
Confronting the Glass Ceiling for Women in the Church
Copyright © 2012 by Danny Silk

Red Arrow Media,
Redding, California

FIRST EDITION

Unless otherwise marked, Scripture quotations are taken from the New King James Version. Copyright © 1982 by Thomas Nelson, Inc. Used by permission. All rights reserved.
Scripture quotations marked MSG are taken from The Message. Copyright © 1993, 1994, 1995, 1996, 2000, 2001, 2002. Used by permission of NavPress Publishing Group.
Scripture quotations marked NASB are taken from the NEW AMERICAN STANDARD BIBLE®, Copyright © 1960,1962,1963,1968,1971,1972,1973,1975,1977,1995 by The Lockman Foundation. Used by permission.
Scripture marked NIV are taken from THE HOLY BIBLE, NEW INTERNATIONAL VERSION®, NIV®. Copyright © 1973, 1978, 1984, 2010 by Biblica, Inc.™ www.xulonpress.com.
Scripture quotations marked RSV are taken from The Holy Bible, The Oxford Annotated Bible, Revised Standard Version Copyright © 1962, by Oxford University Press, Inc., Division of Christian Education of the National Council of Churches of Christ in the United States of America.

Cover Design: © Linda Lee
Interior Design: © Renee Evans

ISBN 10: 0988499207
ISBN 13: 978-0-9884992-0-1
Printed in the United States
redarrowmedia.com

Acknowledgements

Thank you, Heidi Baker, for showing us what a powerful life lives like.

A special thanks to all the ladies who endorsed this book. What we need more than ever today are role models for our young women to aspire to. Thank you all for giving them such hope to find their God-given destiny as leaders in His Church.

Allison Armerding, you've done it again. You've taken something in my heart and helped me put it on display better than I ever could have by myself. I am forever thankful for all your masterful editing and contribution to this work.

Amy Calkins, thank you for doing the heavy lifting on this project. You got this all going for me. I'd still be talking about it if it weren't for you.

The ladies at Red Arrow - Vanessa, Renee, Allison, Amy, and Jessica - you've done such a great job publishing this book. It's even better than I expected, and I expected a lot from you. This book is beautiful! It's been an absolute pleasure to work with you all.

Rich Schmidt you are a true champion for our women. Thank you for all your theological advice and input.

Linda Lee and Myriah Grubbs, thanks for pulling out the stops to get this cover done. I'm in love with it!

A special thanks to all the ladies who exposed their hearts and the men who know how to run alongside their powerful women.

Lani, thanks for making Papa look amazing. I love you!

Contents

"A girl can grow up to be almost anything today—the commander of a NASA space station like Eileen Collins, or Secretary of State like Condoleezza Rice, or a Fortune 500 CEO like Anne Mulcahy of Xerox—but not a minister or even a teacher in some of the larger Christian denominations."

RENA PEDERSON,
PULITZER PRIZE FINALIST AND AUTHOR OF *THE LOST APOSTLE*[1]

Foreword

BY HEIDI BAKER

*D*anny is an amazing leader whose passion for covenant relationships can inspire us all. His heart to see women thrive in their fullest potential is unyielding. I am so thankful he has the courage to honor powerful and anointed women in the Church today. *Powerful and Free* will help liberate women into their true callings. It will also free men from carrying the weight of being both spiritual father and mother. There is a special place for all people within the Body of Christ, regardless of gender, race, ethnicity, or social status. Danny's call in this book, if taken seriously, has the potential to transform the Church and to take God's people to new heights in unity, honor, and love for the glory of God.

Danny recognizes that there is an absence of "female apostolic leaders in America who are leading congregations, denominations, or church networks." He wants to see women emerge in the Church who can be "recognized in a positive light." I also would love to see more women raised up and released within the Church. I grew up without a context for seeing powerful women in the Church. I had not seen any women preachers, so when I received the call to preach at sixteen, I preached to whoever would listen. At that time, this meant preaching on the streets. Since then, I have been shot at, beat up, strangled, ridiculed, had knives to my throat, and imprisoned in three countries. I'm just one tiny little Mama in the dirt who wants to be a carrier of His glory for this generation coming to Jesus. Whatever it might look like, I want God to let His love and His glory shine out of my little laid-down life. As every one of us, male and female, says yes with a yielded cry to God, we will see things shift in the natural and the spiritual realm.

It is remarkable that the very Son of God revealed and humbled Himself by being born inside the womb of a woman. There is also a beautiful participation in Mary, Jesus, the Father, and the Holy Spirit—all saying yes as one. Jesus was dependent upon Mary for life. He did not come out of the womb saying, "Follow me; I am the Son of God." He came out of the womb needy and was nursed at His mother's breast.

Mary had the high calling to release the Son of God. She also had to bear the reproach. She carried a destiny inside of her that was misunderstood. She looked like an unclean woman to the world. Nobody understood her, and yet she said yes to God, so much so that she nurtured her miracle child at a great cost. Many women may feel similar to the way Mary may have felt. Men who sympathize with the way women have been treated over the years may feel it too. Regardless of what people may think, it is important to carry what God has placed inside of us to full term.

God has placed powerful promises and destinies inside both men and women. Now is the time to pay with our hearts, our minds, and our spirits the kind of price that will say yes no matter what it takes. Creating space within the Church for powerful women to shine will be a key to helping launch the Church into its destiny. Let us be a people who say yes to releasing women to fulfill their God given destinies within our generation. Whether we are slandered, ridiculed, persecuted, or even just misunderstood, it is time to go after all that God has for us, whatever that might look like. There may be resistance when releasing powerful women in ministry; however, the rewards will greatly outweigh the costs.

As sons and daughters, let us lay ourselves before Him today and ask Him to meet us in a greater measure. Whether we are rich or poor, live in a mud hut or on Wall Street, are male or female—He wants to break the boxes that limit His Kingdom's expansion in and through our lives. He wants to break our boxes, whatever the size. Whether it is a Baptist or Pentecostal box, a leadership or a gender box, it is a box God wants to break so He can give us more of Himself. We have no clue how glorious, how awesome, and how costly God's call is on our lives. All we really have to do is say yes everyday for the rest of our lives.

As you begin *Powerful and Free*, I want to ask you to pray a really brave prayer. I want to ask you to pray that God would break your box. Whatever your box is for the Christian life—for ministry, for missions, for leadership roles within the Church, whatever you thought it was, whatever you dreamed it was—just ask Him to break it and to give you more of a capacity to carry His glory.

Lord, we don't care what it costs us; we want to say yes to all that You have for us in our generation. We want to carry Your promise. Break our boxes. Crash in on us and give us the tenacity to do what You have asked us to do, to carry the promise that You have put in us to full term. I ask for the miracle of courage to release women in the Church to new levels. I ask for covenant relationships of radical love between husband and wife and male and female. Would You bring even greater unity into the Church for the glory and praise of Your name. May we be a generation that fulfills Your purposes for our lives, regardless of the cost. May You give us courage to rise to new heights for Your glory, shattering any glass ceilings that hold us back from all that You have for us. I pray that *Powerful and Free* will help both women and men step into even more of their amazing, God-given destinies.

Heidi Baker, PhD
FOUNDING DIRECTOR OF IRIS MINISTRIES

Chapter One

THE STORY BEHIND POWERFUL AND FREE

Another December had come to Weaverville, California. I lay in bed awake, watching the snow and dreaming, like any eight-year-old kid, of Santa Claus and my long wish list of toys.

Suddenly, a gurgling, painful cry sounded from the kitchen, jerking me from my reverie. With chest thudding, I crept out of bed and down the hall to investigate.

What I found paralyzed me.

There stood my mother's latest boyfriend, Doug—a six-foot-four, 250-pound behemoth. His huge hands gripped my mother's throat, pinning her petite body to the wall like a rag doll. Her feet dangled inches above the floor.

Doug saw me framed in the doorway. He dropped my mother, who collapsed lifelessly on the linoleum, and turned, wild-eyed, in my direction.

I took off down the hall, scrambled into my bedroom and slammed the door. Trembling, I jumped onto my bed and braced for Doug to burst in.

But he never came. Instead, I made out a muffled rustling coming from my mom's room. The slam of the front door soon followed, and moments later I heard the Volkswagen rev to life, its wheels crunching and skidding on the snow as Doug made his getaway.

When the sound of the engine had faded, I slipped off my bed and ran to the kitchen to see if my mom was alive. She was still lying on the floor where Doug had dropped her, but she was breathing. I watched, petrified, as she came to, coughing and sobbing. Finally, she sat up and looked at me. Neither of us said anything.

Weakly, my mother stood and slowly walked to her room. There she discovered that, along with her car, Doug had stolen her stash of cash for Christmas.

But Doug had robbed us of even more. That night, he ripped the last vestige of safety from our home. That was the night I first tasted terror.

That was the night I first felt powerless.

Sadly, Doug was one in a long parade of men who passed through my childhood as my mother fruitlessly searched for a good partner and father for her boys. My memories of that time have blurred into overlapping, terrifying episodes in which she and a man were screaming, breaking things, and threatening each other while my brother Jonny and I hid, cowering in the next room.

Each of these episodes hammered home the same truth. I was her oldest son. I should have been able to protect her. But I couldn't. I was a child. It didn't matter how much I wanted to protect her or change our circumstances. I could do nothing.

As I grew into an adult, I naturally adopted the belief that survival was my only option. I spent most of my energy escaping those who could abuse me with their power. Meanwhile, I fostered a deep rage in my heart. This rage was my power, and I wielded it against things and people who I knew couldn't fight back—including at times my little brother Jonny, I'm sorry to say.

Then, when I turned twenty-one, God invaded my world. Through a series of miraculous circumstances, I surrendered my life to Jesus Christ. In an instant, hope and expectancy pushed me out of survival mode. The believers I met were also filled with this same hope. I had never known people like this. They expected themselves, and those around them, to be safe, victorious, and powerful. For the first time, I began to believe that I could be someone other than a survivor. I had an extraordinary destiny. Everything was going to be perfect. Or so I thought.

Into the Crucible

Little did I know that unraveling my survival mindset would require a long journey—the journey of learning to love a woman. The first stage in the extraordinary destiny before me was, in essence, to completely reverse my childhood reality of being powerless to protect the most significant woman in my life. And this wasn't going to be easy. As you're about to read, it only took me about a decade! But this journey proved to be the crucible that forged my life message—a message about God's design for Kingdom relationships. This message forms the foundation for everything I teach, including what I have to say about empowering women in the Church.

So let's go back to the beginning of this journey. The woman I'm talking about is, of course, my wife, Sheri. Sheri and I both grew up in Weaverville, went to the same middle school, and met Jesus around the same time at the same church. Once we started to get to know each other, however, it became pretty obvious that this was about all we had in common. Sheri was my opposite—extroverted, ambitious, and influential. Her mom, Norma, once said, "Sheri never met a stranger in her life." At the time, she was already running her own business. This girl was *going places*. And I had no problem with that. So what if I wasn't as driven or outgoing as she was? So what if I was just beginning to set my sights above the line of survival? We both loved Jesus and we loved each other—what else did we need?

You can probably guess what came next. Marrying your opposite only works if you know how to communicate and resolve conflict. Sheri and I both came from families who were clueless on both counts. We grew up playing defense. Intimacy and trust were foreign concepts. We didn't know how to fight for connection and unity in every decision, action, and attitude. Not only that, I simply had no skills for dealing with a strong woman like Sheri. I was used to getting my way in relationships with women. I actually thought I had some kind of magic "happy dust" I could use to make the women in my life happy and get them to go along with whatever I was doing. But "happy dust" didn't work on Sheri. She was adamant that our marriage would not be made up of one person overpowering the other. She insisted that her opinion and voice be validated, and fought to be involved in the vision, decisions, and outcomes of our family.

I only had one grid for understanding Sheri's unrelenting and often angry "pushback." All I could see was that, somehow, the one thing I had been most afraid of in my life before Christ was the very thing I had introduced permanently into my life through marriage—a powerful person who threatened my power. As our relationship became increasingly fraught with conflict, all my old, familiar emotions of powerlessness and rage came back. But this time, I knew I couldn't revert to my "fight or flight" survival tactics. I had made a vow before God to faithfully love and honor Sheri till death do us part. I found myself asking, *What am I going to do? Embracing Christ was so freeing and hopeful. But my marriage is stuck in a war zone. Where do hope and freedom fit in my relationship with Sheri?*

Prior to joining the Church, I had little exposure to chauvinism or male-female hierarchy. My mom was the most influential person in my life, and my world completely lacked strong male figures. But when I found myself desperately searching for "godly" tools to negotiate the unstable power dynamics in my marriage, I stumbled upon the idea that in a Christian marriage, the man is the "head" and the woman is not. No one in the Church actually had to teach me that men were more important, valuable, or powerful than women. I just picked it up by osmosis. It seemed to be the default position of Christian culture. I found what seemed to be obvious verses in the Bible that reinforced this belief—like the verses prohibiting women from talking in church or having authority, and the verses prescribing head coverings and no jewelry. Admittedly, though I later learned there were churches out there actually taking these verses literally, no one I knew did. Women could talk in church, and some women even taught from the front. No women had their heads covered, and most of the women I knew wore jewelry and makeup. Even so, I cherished the covert belief that God wanted me as a man to rule over the woman in my life, and these Scriptures essentially gave me a "final answer" trump card to use as a husband.

The trump card only worked a little better than the happy dust. Sheri knew the Bible verses too, and had a harder time blowing them off. However, it deeply frustrated her to concede this power to me, and it did nothing to help our connection. I remember numerous times when, in the midst of an argument where I was refusing to budge on some final decision I'd made as the "head of the house," Sheri would shout at me, "I know, because you're the man, right?" I could never understand why she was upset. I never felt like I was dominating or heavy-handed in our relationship. I honestly don't remember ever making a decision that didn't include factoring in her needs. Nonetheless, Sheri was uneasy with my veto power and her assigned position of "submission" as a Christian woman.

The fact that she *could* be disregarded in an important decision, simply because of a religious structure that said she had less power than I did, made her uncomfortable and hurt our relationship.

A Better Way

The turning point in our marriage finally came when Sheri scheduled a prayer session with an inner healing and deliverance ministry called Sozo.[1] I was hoping she would come home from the experience and tell me that God had helped her work through some of her issues (oh yes, I was "that" guy). Instead, she announced that, according to the Holy Spirit, the root of most problems in her life was that she had never felt protected—in particular, that *she had never felt protected by me.*

What? Hang on a minute here…could you say that again?

Sheri's revelation rocked me to my core. The idea that I was supposed to protect this powerful and often angry person absolutely baffled me. She had always seemed quite capable of defending herself. *Thank you very much!*

But as crazy as this revelation seemed to me, I couldn't deny that Sheri had legitimately heard from God. I had to acknowledge that God wanted me to make a complete paradigm shift in how I viewed and treated my wife.

After I swallowed this pill, the lights came on for me. I began noticing the many ways in which I consistently maneuvered to protect *myself* when interacting with Sheri, and then saw how these maneuvers created disconnection and discord in our relationship. For example, whenever Sheri and I discussed a problem she was having with someone and I thought Sheri was out of line, I usually ended up defending the other person. Instead of validating her and remaining her loyal ally as a husband, I would identify with those I perceived as her victims and leave her to defend herself. Then, feeling misunderstood, abandoned, and betrayed, she would naturally lash out at me—thereby giving me a reason to pull away even more.

Eventually, the real truth hit me: I had grown up feeling unprotected, and I had married a woman who had grown up feeling unprotected. The only thing we knew how to do was to protect ourselves. And a marriage of two people who are protecting themselves from one another is fundamentally compromised. Though I had pledged Sheri my heart, I had ended up building much of my life around protecting myself—and to some extent, the rest of the world—*from her*. And I needed to stop. We both did. We needed to rebuild our relationship around the priority of protecting one another.

In order to break the cycles of self-protection in our relationship, I had to repent for using my wife's anger as an excuse to move away from her. The only tools I had for dealing with her anger were to deflect it and retreat. Instead of facing my fears and trying to understand and help her, I had built a case, using my position of "headship" and other excuses, to justify withholding myself from her. I had to drop my case and start being a true partner to Sheri—a husband who would offer his strength to her *no matter what*.

When I began trying to move toward Sheri and validate her in the midst of conflict, she initially jabbed back at me even harder to test my resolve. I had to prove that I was going to fight for her, not against her. I had to slay the dragon of her fears and win her heart. As I refused to back down and consistently paid attention to her heart, she gradually stopped displaying the old walls of anger and started showing me what was behind them—a hurting, scared woman who needed my strength, comfort, and friendship. I had the privilege of getting to know a vulnerable, feminine Sheri who not only needed my protection, but who I truly desired to protect.

Learning to protect and move toward my wife required me to access strength inside myself like never before. For the first time in my life, I discovered what it meant for me to become a powerful person: someone who could stand his ground and engage with Sheri's pushback productively— like a weight-trainer working out with weights. I also recognized that I needed to be strong enough to be vulnerable, strong enough to let Sheri in, and strong enough to trust her to protect *my* heart. I needed to carry a high value for her opinion and for what she had to offer me.

Over the next few years, through consistent practice, Sheri and I turned our marriage into a powerful partnership. We learned how to make sure both our voices were heard and our needs met as we made decisions. We learned to "keep our love on" and keep moving toward each other, even when it was scary. We became skilled in making room for one another's strengths, and in covering one another when vulnerabilities were exposed or energies low. And we learned to trust each other to protect our hearts as we pursued growth in our fields and spheres of influence.

And by the way, we tore up my trump card. The male-female hierarchy we'd picked up in the Church effectively made me the only powerful person in our relationship, which hurt both of us. Neither of us could thrive as long as our relationship was built on distrust and power plays rather than connection and power-sharing. With my trump card, I had unknowingly recreated for Sheri the very scenario of powerlessness I had experienced as a boy—and it needed to go. Thankfully, the Kingdom of Heaven invaded our marriage and taught us a better way.

Seeking a Consistent Kingdom Paradigm

Sheri and I have been living and teaching this better way around the globe for over a decade. Imparting a Kingdom vision for powerful partnerships to the Body of Christ turned out to be the second stage in the destiny God initiated when He took hold of my life. Wonderfully, as we have passed on the truths, tools, and core values that transformed our marriage and family, we have seen that transformation repeated in countless lives. But in the process, a new stage of our destiny has emerged. Sheri and I have found ourselves not only addressing the relational dynamics in marriages and families, but also the corporate dynamics of the Church and society.

This stage, in part,[2] began as we experienced a real dissonance—not only between the traditional male-female hierarchy in Christian marriages and our message of strong, equal, male-female partnerships, but also between that message and the reality that men and women are nowhere near equal in power in church leadership. We discovered that there is a direct ideological and cultural connection between marriage hierarchy and the Church's male-dominant leadership. Both realities work together to send a structural message about gender to the Body of Christ. Sheri and I began to see that no matter how much we teach men and women to have strong partnerships in marriage, believers and churches will be limited in their ability to express real gender equality and partnership in every area if our leadership structure is not also expressing it.

This experience was personal, to say the least. Sheri and I are both church leaders. The contrast between my reality as a leader and my wife's reality was impossible to ignore. Now, *please hear me*. I am the first to say that our home, Bethel Church, is one of the most free and empowering churches on the planet. We firmly believe in the equality of men and women before God, and empowering women has been on our agenda for a while. Yet the very reason I have written this book is that even a free and powerful church like Bethel has not escaped the cultural norm of male-dominant leadership—not to mention most of the churches with which we are connected—and many ladies have been hitting the glass ceiling as a result.

Both Sheri and I are fully aware that no one person or church is responsible for this norm. As we will explore in the next chapter, it is simply the drift of our fallen human nature. You don't really need to learn it; you can just drink it in the water. But my wife was born to stir the waters. Sheri brought the same passion for equality and power-sharing to her position of leadership that she brought to our marriage. And it was as she struggled to "happen" as a leader that we started noticing how common her situation was. We noticed that there were virtually no women in the senior leadership teams of the churches in our movement—actual leaders, not just wives of leaders. We heard countless stories of powerful and gifted women who desired to serve the Church, but had finally given up to pursue opportunities in other fields where they could reach their potential and not be relegated to "women's ministry." There was a wide gap between the accounts we received from the male pastors who affirmed that women were empowered in their churches and the accounts we received from the women in their churches who admitted to feeling unseen, unheard, and undervalued.

We also started to become aware of how male-dominant leadership was limiting church growth and forfeiting the benefits gifted women have to offer the Body. I remember sitting next to a woman at a leadership conference who told me she was a hospital director. As she described the demands of her job, it was immediately apparent that I was sitting next to a woman with incredible intelligence and leadership skills. She then proceeded to tell me that she had been trying to get more involved at her church, and had been directed to participate in a women's committee. At the first committee meeting she attended, the ladies spent nearly a third of the time discussing napkin arrangements for an upcoming church function. As the meeting wrapped up, this woman leaned over to a friend and said,

"Well, I won't be coming to any more of these meetings."

I can't tell you how many stories I've heard like this. What does it say about the Church when we send professional women to work on napkin arrangements instead of, say, on the church board? At the very least, I think it says we are *missing out*.

Kris Vallotton and I have both been going after this issue when we minister to leaders in churches. Several years ago, Kris and I travelled to speak at a particular church, and on the first night of our stay, we had dinner with the pastor and his wife. Partway through the meal, Kris pointed his finger at the wife, who was a very radical believer, but also a very soft-spoken woman. He said, "I'm really impressed with you! Why aren't you occupying your place of authority in this environment?"

"I don't know what you mean," she said.

"The Lord has shown me that you are to be promoted to co-labor with your husband and share the authority in this environment," Kris continued.

She looked at her husband.

He looked at her. Then he looked at Kris and asked, "What does that mean?"

"I don't know," Kris answered honestly.

The next day, we met with the elders of the church to discuss various issues. One of the issues they brought up was that their growth had been constrained for several years. We began to ask more questions and discovered that they had a very apostolic and prophetic environment in their church. Signs and wonders were happening, prophetic teams were ministering accurately, and people were being attracted to the supernatural environment. The problem was, people weren't feeling pastored. They weren't feeling nurtured or connected, and so they weren't staying.

After listening to their explanation, Kris asked, "Where are the women in your leadership?"

The elders looked at each other in surprise. It was all men in the room. They had *no* female leaders. The pastor spoke up. "I've been here for seventeen years, and we've never had women at this level."

Kris looked pointedly at him. "You have no powerful women here on purpose, and that is the reason for your constraint. You have no women at the top levels of authority, influence, and decision-making in your environment. When you remove the woman from a family, the quality of her presence is removed from that family."

This is the structural message and reality I'm talking about. I'm not saying that all women contribute a "pastoral" element to churches *per se*. I am saying that, in the same way a Kingdom marriage requires a powerful man and a powerful woman, a Kingdom church culture requires powerful men and powerful women partnering in church leadership at every level. And right now, we don't have them. Instead, we have a male-dominant leadership structure that continues to send a message to the Church that women aren't as valuable, gifted, or anointed as men.

In *Powerful and Free*, we will journey into some of the primary reasons for this problem. Lack of awareness is a big one. Many believers are completely unconscious of their own gender bias and where it comes from. They're not aware of what it's really like for women to lead in the Church and encounter the glass ceiling. They don't know what the Bible actually teaches about "headship," "submission," and women having "authority." They don't have a clear vision of God's design for gender, or a vision for powerful male-female partnerships. And they don't know where to begin taking steps to turn the tide. All of these, and more, are covered in the pages ahead.

What Does it Mean to be Powerful and Free?

Before we move into those pages, however, I want to close this chapter with a brief explanation of the title of this book. *Powerful* and *free* are terms that have often been misunderstood or misused in Western culture. *Gender equality* is another term that has picked up some not-so-positive associations. True equality, power, and freedom, as Sheri and I discovered in our marriage, only exist in the context of Kingdom relationships.

Equality in Kingdom relationships flows from the recognition of how deeply God values us. Our value is defined by the price Jesus paid to redeem and restore us as equal sons and daughters of God. This worth cannot be added to or diminished by any human action. If we think that age, sin, gender, economic status, ethnic background, or any other characteristic changes a person's value (or our own) and excuses us from treating them like Christ treats them, we forfeit our ability to experience Kingdom partnerships and relationships.

Human beings tend to devalue themselves and one another when they're afraid. Fear is the enemy of love, freedom, and power. It is the destroyer of relationships—it divides and separates. Fear is largely responsible for the unhealthy dynamics that arise in families and church cultures. When we are confronted with people who scare us, fear makes it difficult for us to remember that they are worthy of love. But Jesus, who never let fear overpower Him, constantly showed us who was worthy—enemies, children, sinners, women, extorters, prostitutes, soldiers, politicians, the sick and diseased, high class, low class, religious, nonreligious. Everyone. He didn't just declare this value either; He honored it by loving *all* of us. And in loving us, He removed every barrier and dividing wall in His way, including the ultimate barriers: sin and death.

This is what God's love does—it casts out fear and destroys every dividing wall created by fear. It heals all disconnection between God and His children, and between each of His sons and daughters. It convinces us of our equal, eternal value and drives us courageously and unstoppably *toward one another*.

Love, by nature, requires *freedom*. Many of us understand that God gave us free will because He desired us to share in mutual, loving relationships with Him and one another. But what we don't always understand is that love is the *whole purpose* for freedom. Freedom is not the license to do whatever we want; freedom is the choice to love. Thus, as soon as we use our freedom to violate love, we lose our freedom and invite bondage into our lives. Galatians 5:13-15 puts it this way:

> *It is absolutely clear that God has called you to a free life. Just make sure that you don't use this freedom as an excuse to do whatever you want to do and destroy your freedom. Rather, use your freedom to serve one another in love; that's how freedom grows. For everything we know about God's Word is summed up in a single sentence: Love others as you love yourself. That's an act of true freedom. If you bite and ravage each other, watch out—in no time at all you will be annihilating each other, and where will your precious freedom be then?* (MSG)

The mark of a truly free person is one who can make and sustain a commitment to love people, especially in long-term covenant relationships. Sheri and I experienced this as we rebuilt our marriage with Heaven's paradigm. Nothing identifies a free choice better than stripping it of everything warm and fuzzy and realizing that it is simply the right thing to do, whether it's comfortable or not. When we were both able to make that free choice, it convinced us we loved each other and laid an unshakable foundation for our connection.

And once again, Sheri and I discovered that exercising our freedom to move toward each other was the key to becoming truly *powerful*. A person who can say, "I'm going to be okay and keep moving toward you no matter what you do," is a powerful person. That person is accessing the only source of true power in the universe—God's love—and is using it as it was designed to be used, thus causing that power to mature and increase. A person who retreats from relationships, passively submits to disconnected relationships, or selfishly dominates relationships is not powerful. That person is forfeiting their power or grasping at false power (such as anger or rage), which can only backfire on them.

If our churches and homes are not sending a message of eternal value to people by loving them and empowering them to "happen," then we are not bringing the Kingdom. If our churches and homes are not cultivating freely chosen partnerships between powerful people who are driven by their hearts' desire and commitment to love, honor, and strengthen one another, then we are not bringing Heaven to earth—which happens to be our mandate.

I truly believe that now is the time to rise up as champions for powerful women and powerful partnerships between men and women. In 2009, not long after the deaths of Jill Austin and Michael Ann Goll, James Goll released this prophetic word:

> Women in ministry and leadership will be released globally across the body of Christ. The two righteous seeds of Michel Ann Goll and Jill Austin have been sown into the ground and there will be a harvest of women in both spiritual and secular leadership arising to be champions of the poor, injustice, prayer, and creativity flowing freely as the prophetic anointing increases in Jesus' name.[3]

For so long, only the men have been free and powerful, but we are beginning to hear the reverberation of freedom for women in the Church. It is only a matter of time until the empowerment of women becomes unstoppable and many of them begin to lead side by side with the men. For my part, I want to be on the front lines of this charge, not reluctantly dragging along at the rear. I want to be a man who believes in the destiny of the women around me and who works hard to protect them from the traditions and people who would hold them back. I want to be part of God's strategy that will bring an unprecedented invasion of Heaven on earth.

Chapter Two

KNOW THY PLACE

*J*ohn Alvarez, chairman of the board of Walnut Evangelical Church, crossed the parking lot and quickly opened his car door. He had just finished the worst board meeting of his life. His suggestion to hire Donna Kline to lead the church's long-term outreach to Indonesia had initiated a throw-down between the old guard, who wanted "their man," Paul Gates, for the position, and the new crew, who seemed open to evaluate other qualified candidates. When one of the new guys brought up the fact that Paul's leadership skills seemed lacking and that a few of his references had alluded to character issues, while Donna had no such issues, yelling and chest-beating erupted. Two longstanding board members threatened to resign in protest. At the end of the meeting, the board narrowly selected Paul over Donna.

As he put his key in the ignition, John suddenly caught sight of Donna. *What was she doing here?* She was sitting in her silver Mini Cooper, her head sunk on the steering wheel. *She already knows.* John felt helpless. He knew it was her dream to go to Indonesia and that she was perfect for the job. But what could he do? Lacking the energy to try and console her, John turned the key and drove home.

That evening, several board members' wives telephoned John's wife to complain about the board's decision. She, in turn, gave him an earful for not taking a stronger stand for Donna in the meeting. Exhausted, he went to bed early, but he slept fitfully. He even had a nightmare that a tremendous lightning bolt struck the church building, causing it to split in two.

When he woke the next morning, he issued a groan. "God help me!" His head ached. He stared at the ceiling and rehearsed, yet again, the contentious meeting. The only conclusion he could reach was that Donna, clearly being the superior candidate, had only lost the vote because she was a "she." Then a thought hit him like a brick: *There are many women in the Church with real insight, leadership skills, and anointing. They contribute much, yet something holds them in check. Something in the Church is keeping called and qualified women from being seen and invited into leadership.*

Immediately, many of the confusing and often contradictory verses about women in the Bible rose from memory to deepen his turmoil. *But what about the man being the "head" of the woman? Is this why men have access to more authority? Does this imply men are superior to women?* His experience told him everyone would benefit from of having women in leadership, but in the end, he didn't have a reasonable theological basis for whether God wanted him to cut against the grain of the established order.

The image of Donna weeping in her car came back to him. *That's it,* John thought. *It's time to get some answers.* He got out of bed, quickly shaved and dressed, and drove to the local Christian bookstore on Highway 73.

A young woman stood behind the counter. Their eyes met, and John smiled. *Perfect!* He thought. *Surely she can help.*

"Good morning," she offered enthusiastically. "Can I help you?"

"Yes, actually," John replied. "I am looking for a book on women in ministry. What do you have?"

She paused. "Do you mean missionary books?"

"No," he said. "I'm looking for scholarly books on God's place for women in ministry and leadership."

"Oh, sorry," she responded, "We don't have anything like that. Most women know their place."

John bit deeply into his lip. Without another word, he left the store, the bell clanging loudly behind him. He climbed back into his car and put the key in the ignition, but didn't turn it.

"I can't believe it!" he said out loud. "Does she really believe that?"

He would never know. But what he *did* know was that his search for the truth had suddenly taken on a deep sense of urgency.

What Lies Beneath

Though the above story is fictional, parts of it are based on the real experiences of a friend of mine. And the idea of a woman having a "place" is anything but fiction. In fact, it is thriving in the Western Church today. Some churches define this place with explicit teaching. Others don't really talk about it—it's just what's expected.

I want to give you a quick and easy tool to identify what you believe (or may not know you believe) about where women belong. It's a tool I learned about in Malcolm Gladwell's book, *Blink*, called an Implicit Association Test (IAT). An Implicit Association Test measures our subconscious associations with characteristics like gender or race.[1] Our brains move quite a bit slower when we have to associate a quality or role with a gender or race that we don't typically associate with that gender or race, making it easy for psychologists to measure what is "normal" for us. I've adapted the IAT Malcolm Gladwell used in *Blink* in order for you to measure your "normal" when it comes to male and female roles in the Church. As Gladwell explains, the IAT is not necessarily a reflection on our consciously chosen beliefs. Rather, it reveals what we unconsciously believe due to what we have picked up from life experiences, education, and culture.[2]

To begin the test, check off whether you think the role in the middle column belongs on the right or the left column in the box below. Work your way down until you reach the end.

MALE or CHURCH LEADER		FEMALE or CHURCH EMPLOYEE
	Apostle	
	Sunday School Teacher	
	Pastor	
	Worship Minister	
	Teacher	
	Small Group Leader	
	Nursery Worker	
	Greeter	

	Treasurer	
	Office Administrator	
	Board Member	
	Marriage Counselor	
	Youth Leader	
	Intercessor	

Okay, now take the test again. Note that the genders are reversed.

FEMALE or CHURCH LEADER		MALE or CHURCH EMPLOYEE
	Apostle	
	Sunday School Teacher	
	Pastor	
	Worship Minister	
	Teacher	
	Small Group Leader	
	Nursery Worker	
	Greeter	
	Treasurer	
	Office Administrator	
	Board Member	
	Marriage Counselor	
	Youth Leader	
	Intercessor	

Okay. How easy was it for you to put "apostle" in the "Female or Church Leader" category? How easy was it for you to put "nursery worker" in the "Male or Church Employee" category? If you are like most, it was a little tricky. We tend to put certain roles with certain genders, and it takes us a lot longer to process when those roles and genders are switched up. It messes with our whole—and mostly unconscious—paradigm of what people are supposed to do.

Male figures dominate our paradigm of what church leadership should look like. It's so normal that we don't even notice it—except when we experience something that may be a bit new to us. For example, a woman with gifts of leadership or teaching, especially one who isn't married to a pastor, tends to stand out in the crowd. Incidentally, when I travel and speak on the issue of women in Church leadership, I like to take a quick poll of how many women in the audience are not married to pastors or leaders but who feel a strong call on their lives to lead. Usually, about thirty percent of the room responds in the affirmative.

Women who want to lead are out there—we just don't realize it. Unless they assert themselves, they tend to remain invisible. And they only assert themselves when they realize that it's going to be a cold day in you-know-where before the Church calls them out to do what God has gifted them to do. No one notices and offers them the opportunity to grow. They have to speak up and ask for it, and in many cases, those conversations don't go too well. When they try to leave their "place," challenging the "normal," it puts some people on the defense. This is when people start hunting around for reasons—especially reasons they can claim are endorsed by God—why "normal" is the way it should be.

The Bible is the first place people look to find those reasons. Many self-appointed "place" police have eagerly pulled out verses that seem tailor-made for telling women where they belong—most of which come from Paul's letters: *"I do not permit a woman to teach or to have authority over a man, but to be in silence"* (1 Tim. 2:12). *"Let your women keep silent in the churches...for it is shameful for women to speak in church"* (1 Cor. 14:-35).

Many feel Paul's black-and-white statements are sufficient to support their position—I know I did when I was first married—but if they happen to want more biblical support for their "place" case, they can certainly dredge up more (we'll be looking at some of these controversial verses later in the book).

And then, of course, there is history. The past few thousand years are loaded with traditions and practices calculated to keep women powerless. Plato, Aristotle, St. Augustine, Thomas Aquinas, Martin Luther, and John Knox are remarkable examples of female place-keepers. I mean, look at the sort of things these guys had to say about women:

Plato: "Females are inferior in goodness to males." [3]

Aristotle: The male is by nature superior and the female inferior, the male ruler and the female subject."[4]

John Knox: "Woman in her greatest perfection was made to serve and obey man."[5]

Thomas Aquinas: "The woman is subject to the man, on account of the weakness of her nature, both of mind and of body…Woman is in subjection according to the law of nature, but a slave is not. Children ought to love their father more than their mother."[6]

Martin Luther: "Men have broad shoulders and narrow hips, and accordingly they possess intelligence. Women have narrow shoulders and broad hips. Women ought to stay home; the way they were created indicates this, for they have broad hips and a wide fundament to sit upon, keep house and bear and raise children."[7]

St. Augustine: "What is the difference whether it is in a wife or a mother; it is still Eve the temptress that we must be aware of in any woman…I fail to see what use women can be to man, if one excludes the function of bearing children."[8]

Sure, such blatantly sexist statements are ridiculous and no longer politically correct. And Paul's instructions about women keeping silent aren't usually applied literally anymore. Yet below the surface, many—women included—still feel something akin to what these guys felt: *It's not natural for a woman to be in leadership. She is built to follow. She is built to be at home. She has a place, and it's not up front…unless she's standing beside a powerful man.*

This feeling persists despite the fact that some of the world's most memorable political leaders have been women. Margaret Thatcher, Golda Meir, Queen Elizabeth, Queen Victoria, and Deborah come to mind. Yet, even with women getting the vote and better access to education and pay, this gut feeling about a woman's place runs deep in our culture. Think about it. Americans were ready for a black president before they were ready for a female president. They were ready to give the black *man* the opportunities and resources to be groomed for that role and were ready to sit under his influence before they were ready to do the same for a woman. The higher the position of leadership, the more we can bet on it being held by a man. The same goes for the Church. How many churches can you think of where the senior pastor is a woman? My guess is you can count the number on one hand. Men hold top-tier leadership positions in local churches and denominations almost exclusively. And it's always been that way, so it feels natural. We are comfortable with the system. It's just the way it is.

Fear and Shame

Where did we develop this "natural" feeling toward women? Why do men almost exclusively control the top tier? Did God really design men to hold the reins? Or is there another thought that can shift the system?

I believe there is.

But I also think that believing it "unnatural" for women to be in leadership is actually a natural feeling that stems from what the Fall did to our views on gender.

What was Adam's response when God unveiled Eve? Was there any hint that he saw her as "Eve the temptress"? Do we find any phrase insinuating that the only thing Eve was good for was to breed little Adams?

Nope. What Adam actually said is beautiful poetry—the first poetry in history for that matter—and it was directed at a companion and friend: *"Finally! Bone of my bone, flesh of my flesh! Name her Woman, for she was made from Man"* (Gen. 2:23 MSG).

Adam instantly recognized Eve as his complementary equal. Moreover, as David J. Hamilton notes in *Why Not Women?*, "God didn't give man dominion over the earth until woman was standing beside him."[9] It was a joint commission. They understand that they were indispensible partners in fulfilling God's command to fill and subdue the earth. There was no question as to whether or not they carried equal value, equal authority, or equal purpose. Of course they did—it was *natural* for them to think that way. They were *one*, after all.

It was only after they sinned that the natural turned unnatural: *"Then the Lord God called to Adam and said to him, 'Where are you?' So he said, 'I heard Your voice in the garden, and I was afraid because I was naked; and I hid myself"* (Gen. 3:9-10). When they sinned, Adam and Eve's natural state—nakedness—

produced fear and shame. Shame is different than guilt. Guilt is that painful feeling we get when we *do* something wrong. Shame is the painful feeling that *we* are wrong.

Adam's response to this pain was to hide and create distance between him and the one who had seen his nakedness—Eve. When God questioned him, he began to blame Eve for his pain— *"The woman whom You gave to be with me…"* (Gen. 3:12). And after God cursed the ground and Adam's labors— *"because you have heeded the voice of your wife"* (Gen. 3:17)—the disconnection between Adam and Eve became an institution. You can almost hear Adam thinking, *I'm never listening to that woman again.*

The first couple then had to figure out a way to cooperate—in uncharted, hostile territory—right after showing each other that they couldn't be trusted. What emerged was the exact opposite of the perfect partnership they shared in Eden. We already know, thanks to my early years of marriage, that disconnected, scared, and shame-filled people working together create endless problems because they use their power to *self-protect* (through hiding, denial, and abandonment) and *control* (through rage, violence, and manipulation) rather than to strengthen and protect each other. What's worse, God told Adam and Eve who would get the upper hand in these power struggles: *"To the woman He said…'Your desire shall be for your husband, and he shall rule over you'"* (Gen. 3:16).

We see these broken dynamics playing out immediately after the Fall in Genesis 4. The theme of this chapter could be dubbed, "Kill your rivals, protect your stuff, and possess your women." Cain kills Abel and then builds a city to protect his stuff (see Gen. 4: 8-17). And then a couple of generations later, Lamech kills a man and institutes polygamy—one of the most notoriously oppressive realities for women in history (see Gen 4:19-24). This pattern of men using violence to gain and preserve power, whether political, military, economic, or sexual, is what I call the *patriarchal paradigm*, and this is the paradigm of every culture throughout history. We all know how it works:

"Might makes right."

"Whoever has the gold rules."

"Survival of the fittest."

It's the law of the jungle that says, "If you threaten anything I control, I will persecute you. I will hurt you. And even kill you if I have to."

When physical strength determines who has the power, the big contest is never between men and women. Let's face it—men *are* physically stronger. The contest is really between strong men and stronger men. This is why government, for millennia, has "naturally" been male, violent, and oppressive. What society across the globe has ever been free from men fighting each other for control? That is the glory of the patriarchal paradigm: Men get to put everyone and everything in their place—specifically the place where they can be controlled, used, and dominated. And they will fight to the death to put them there.

That is how God's prophecy to Eve about "her husband ruling her" came down to basically mean that men would determine the place of women. And according to the logic of the patriarchal paradigm, women—by virtue of their anatomy and the fact that they happen to be weakest and most vulnerable (and thus most easily controlled) when they do what they alone can do—bear children—clearly belong in one place doing one thing. And that place is at home and that thing is having babies and serving men. This seemed so "normal" and "natural" that it came to be seen as a law of nature, like gravity.

The Anti-Patriarch

It is easy to believe and preach that hierarchy—the patriarchal paradigm—is what God always had in mind. People expect God to dominate with His power. And they often think they can use His power to dominate others. Tyrants, conquerors, and cult leaders all work to convince people that they speak for God, or that they are God, in order to secure their position.

With that, it's fairly common for people to read the Old Testament as the record of God's patriarchal exploits, stepping in to wipe out Israel's enemies and fulfill her destiny to conquer and dominate the Promised Land. But a closer look reveals something different. That something is a God who was always inviting Israel into a covenant relationship based on mutual love and faithfulness—a covenant where He instructed them in anti-patriarchal practices like giving equal honor to fathers and mothers and caring for the weak members of society, such as widows and orphans. In Isaiah 58, for example, God told the Israelites that a *true* fast is one where the oppressor's yoke is broken, the subjugated set free, the naked clothed, and the hungry fed. It was the Israelites who were continually pulling away from God toward the patriarchal paradigm, demanding that God give them kings so they had a man at the top to compete with surrounding nations (even though God warned them explicitly about the negative effects of having a king—see 1 Samuel 8). And then Israel's intelligentsia spent a few hundred years building up volumes of interpretations of the Law to excuse divorce, polygamy, slavery, racism, and other forms of oppression and injustice. None of those ideas were God's. They all came from men.

Well, God gave them what they wanted: a king. And the Israelites got exactly what they asked for—centuries of political upheaval that ended in losing their precious kingdom altogether. After that, their only hope was that God would raise up a mighty king, the Messiah, to reclaim Israel's rightful place at the top of the hierarchy as the people of the one true God. They were looking for the ultimate strong man—a military leader who would cast off their oppressors and usher in a Golden Age of political power.

Israel never dreamed her Messiah would come as the Suffering Servant— the ultimate anti-patriarch. At every turn, Jesus dismantled the logic of the patriarchal paradigm, exposing it to be absolutely contrary to God's nature and design for humanity. He said:

> *You know that the rulers of the Gentiles lord it over them, and those who are great exercise authority over them. Yet it shall not be so among you; but whoever desires to become great among you, let him be your servant. And whoever desires to be first among you, let him be your slave—just as the Son of Man did not come to be served, but to serve, and to give His life a ransom for many.* (Matt. 20:25-28)

This statement was a major "does not compute" for His disciples—not to mention the religious leaders of the day. Jesus confounded the world by becoming a servant. Not only did the most powerful Person in the universe use His power to raise up those around Him, rather than dominate them, but He also raised up those who everyone knew belonged at the bottom of the social heap. These were the "natural" lowlifes—the lepers, the children, the demon-possessed, the women, the Samaritans, the tax collectors, the sinners. He was always messing with the "place" assigned to them. More often than not, He did that by joining them wherever that "place" was. He went where no respectable rabbi had gone before.

There were many places women did not belong in first century Jewish culture. They especially didn't belong anywhere religious education took place—in the inner courts of the Temple, the main area of the synagogue, or sitting at a rabbi's feet. Women had to pick up whatever teaching they could from behind screens or at home with their husbands. One of the rabbinical laws of the day stated, "Let the words of the Law be burned rather than committed to women... If a man teaches his daughter the Law, it is as though he taught her lewdness."[10]

Jesus defied all of these rules.

He taught in the outer courts of the Temple so women could join the audience. He called a crippled woman forward in the synagogue—into the men's area—and healed her (see Luke:13:10-17). He told Martha that Mary's place was at His feet and not in the kitchen (see Luke 10:42). Jesus included women among His disciples and ministry team, touched and healed their bodies, let them touch Him, spoke to them with honor and praise, taught that they were equal partners in marriage and deserved justice, protected them from accusation, forgave their sins, and showed them affection and love.[11]

Perhaps the most astounding account of the "place" Jesus gave to women is found in the story of the Samaritan woman in John 4. Jesus approaches the woman at the well and asks her for water. Already we know something is up. A Jewish man never would have spoken publically to a woman, much less to a Samaritan woman, and even less to a Samaritan woman with a past like this one's. Not only does Jesus talk with her, but He also talks with her about theology—a topic expressly forbidden to discuss with women. In one conversation, Jesus literally sliced through years of rabbinical law and cultural norms with the extreme love of God that sees the treasure in every human heart.[12]

Nevertheless, as David J. Hamilton notes, this conversation is remarkable for more than its many violations of the status quo. It is Jesus's longest one-on-one dialogue, and in it He reveals for the first time that He is the long awaited Messiah. That's right—Jesus revealed who He was to a Samaritan woman with a history as long as your phone book before he revealed it to His disciples.[13]

After Jesus entrusted her with this revelation, He didn't say, "Well, I've already broken enough rules by teaching you this stuff. It's okay for women to learn, but it stops here—you can learn, but you can't teach." He let her carry the message back to town, and stayed two more days to back up her testimony. She was, in essence, one of the first missionaries. And she was someone whose designated "place" was in the reject pile.

Jesus entrusted another major message—the testimony of His resurrection—to a woman, Mary Magdalene (see John 20:1-18). Mary was not the only person standing around the tomb—both Peter and John showed up and looked inside—but Jesus didn't appear until they had gone. He chose a woman as the *first* witness of His resurrected body. Significantly, one of the proofs theologians offer for the legitimacy of the testimony of Christ's resurrection in the Gospels is the fact it originated with women.[14] In first century Roman and Jewish society, a woman's testimony was worth nil. If you wanted people to believe something you were telling them, you would *never* have said that you heard it from a woman. The only reason the Gospel writers would have faithfully recorded that the testimony came from Mary was because it was true.

Christ commissioning Mary to announce His resurrection was a sign of what He had just accomplished through His suffering, death, and resurrection, and that was the fact that He had uprooted the patriarchal paradigm once and for all. As He hung naked on the cross, Jesus transferred sin (the source of Adam's fear and shame) onto Himself. Instead of hiding, blaming, and self-protecting, He willingly died as a guilty man in plain sight before God and humanity.

Jesus completely disempowered the spiritual forces that had been turning the wheels of fear, shame, and oppression since the Fall. He reclaimed the usurped authority the enemy used to trick people into using their power to control and dominate rather than serve and strengthen. Jesus buried Adam's fallen nature in the grave and rose with a new nature. This new nature, which He generously shares with us, enables us to love and live as He does. It allows us to overcome fear with love, sacrifice our self-interest, and move toward one another even when we mess up.

Perhaps most amazing of all, Jesus ascended to the Father and gave us all a new *place* in relationship with Him. He told Mary, "*...go to My brethren and say to them, 'I am ascending to My Father and your Father, and to My God and your God'*" (John 20:17). He was saying, "I want you to know your place. *My place is now your place.* My relationship with the Father is now your relationship with the Father. You are His sons and daughters, My brothers and sisters." It was only appropriate that Jesus commission a formerly demon-possessed, outcast woman as His first apostle to announce that patriarchy had received its deathblow and a new kingdom of freedom, love, and restoration had been established.

2,000 Years Later

It's been 2,000 years since Mary announced that we are not only brothers and sisters *in* Christ, but also brothers and sisters *of* Christ, sharing equal standing and value before the Father. It's been 2,000 years since God gave us a new nature—His nature—and forever redefined what was "natural" for us, particularly in our relationships.

It is no longer natural for the strong to dominate the weak. It is natural for the strong to strengthen the weak. It is no longer natural to strive to be king of the hill. It is natural to seek the lowest place in order to lift others up, just like the members of the Trinity. It is no longer natural to "put" people in their place. It is natural to empathize and identify with people in order to love, encourage, and empower them.

And it is no longer natural to view women—or anyone for that matter—as unfit to lead or fill any role in the Body of Christ on the basis of gender, marital status, economic status, ethnic background, or any physical or material characteristic. It is natural for us to recognize our leaders *solely* on the basis of their anointing, gifts, calling, and character. But tragically, after 2,000 years, many of us are still wearing the grave clothes of fear and shame that keep us from fully expressing our new "natural."

The Church should be the safest, freest, and most empowering place for women—for anyone. It should be a place where God can show off by taking the world's rejects and revealing the incredible gifts, beauty, and power He has placed within them. But the fact remains that the patriarchal paradigm still exists in the Church. And consequently, we don't give people, including female leaders, the place they deserve. Ultimately, it keeps us from receiving the wealth of benefits they have to offer.

Chapter Three

THE REALITY OF THE GLASS CEILING

A young woman I know spent several summers during her college years working at a Christian youth camp. One summer, she was the only female on the camp's summer staff leadership team. Though she held one of the highest positions of authority on the team, she felt frustrated by her lack of influence. It seemed like most of the staff under her didn't take her seriously. When she asked them to improve their game or do a better job following the rules, she noticed no real change in their behavior. The male leaders didn't have the same problem motivating the staff, and this bothered her.

One night, the eight leaders were having some team-building time over dinner. As the men joked back and forth, one of them offhandedly commented that men don't really care what women think of them. This caught my friend's attention. "What do you mean?" she asked, thinking he was teasing.

"A man only cares about what a woman thinks of him if he's interested in dating her," another guy explained, in all seriousness. "Otherwise, he only cares what other men think of him."

"What?" my friend said in disbelief. "That's not fair! Women care about what everyone thinks about them—even people they don't like."

The men looked at each other and shrugged. "That's just how it is," one of them said.

The conversation moved on, but my friend had stopped listening. *This explains so much*, she thought. *They don't listen to me because they don't care what I think of them.*

Unfortunately, this thought failed to dawn on the men around the table. They remained oblivious to the injustice of the message hidden in their words. They had no idea they were kicking my friend to the curb. Having been taught all sorts of debilitating beliefs about female submission and male authority growing up, she was not yet confident enough to confront her male peers and reject the powerlessness placed on her that evening. Though she had received a revelation about the limitations that were keeping her from having real authority in her leadership position, it was not until several years later that she began to realize that "the way it is" isn't the way it has to be.

Over and over again, women in our churches have received the same type of message capping their value and influence. Even in the freest of church environments, women are still banging their heads on a *glass ceiling*: "an intangible barrier within a hierarchy that prevents women or minorities from obtaining upper-level positions."[1] Or, like my friend, some women may have a position of leadership, but are not able to operate in that position to their potential because people do not value or receive their authority and influence. Many men don't notice this glass ceiling in the Church, however, because it's not intended to hold them back. They glide right through it, thinking, *Women are empowered in my church. I let my wife be powerful.* The truth is that many men are completely blind to the experiences of women in the Church. They either still think women belong in a "submissive" role, or they think equality is already a reality. Either way, they see no real need for change. They are content with how it's always been.

I want to challenge this contentment and call us to do better. I think we as the Body of Christ are missing out on what our female leaders have to offer. But in order to create and deepen our value for female leaders, we first need to be willing to listen to them tell us what it's like to be women leading in the Church. We need to hear them talk about the glass ceiling. And we need to challenge ourselves not to invalidate or write off what they are telling us.

In order to help us do that, I interviewed a handful of powerful women in the Church. Each would describe herself as a strong woman with excellent leadership abilities and a desire to be an influential and powerful person. These women all hold positions of leadership, either in the Church or outside the Church, and some of them are leaders in both arenas. They range in age from thirty to sixty, represent different ethnic groups, have worked in a variety of fields, and vary greatly in education and experience. Yet all of them are closely acquainted with the glass ceiling.

Most of them would not feel safe sharing their thoughts and experiences candidly with the general public. They have shared them with me so that I can give you a perspective you may never hear from a woman face-to-face—not because it's not true, but because many women in the Church do not feel safe enough to tell the *whole* truth. They do not believe the men in their lives want to hear or are willing to accept the reality of what it feels like to be a woman in the Church. They have been criticized, ignored, and patronized—yet their dreams still burn within them. Some are determined to "happen," even if they need to trade the Church for the marketplace to do it. Others have simply resigned themselves to "the way it's always been." These women are not complainers. They are not victims who find their identity in what others have done to them or kept from them. Nonetheless, at the risk of sounding negative, they have agreed to be vulnerable and honest enough to share their experiences with me. Here are their thoughts and stories.[2]

Leading as a Woman

Elizabeth, founder and executive director of an international parachurch ministry, credits much of her success to the male leaders who have persistently supported her and her ministry. However, she admits to wrestling with feeling like she has second-class status and limited opportunities as a woman within the Church. It seems to her that she somehow puts off the senior level "men's club," for they have always found reasons not to work with her. The glass ceiling feels real to her, and she admits that she needs to manage her heart to guard against offense. She wonders whether the limits she experiences have to do with her age, her particular area of gifting, or the fact that she is a woman.

Marjorie, a leader at a Christian educational institution, has had many painful experiences in the Church. At one church (which she no longer attends) she was told that she must get rid of her "Eve nature" and that nothing could come from her or any other woman without it first going through a man. She was taught that a woman could only be in ministry if her husband balanced out her "extreme" and "unbalanced" tendencies as a woman. A church leader once told her husband, "If you don't take control of your wife, you'll never go anywhere in your call from God." Because of her strong leadership gift and personality and her commitment to excellence, Marjorie has, at least once, been labeled a "Jezebel," though she is neither rebellious nor subversive. And she experienced physically violent abuse from church leaders demanding she "submit"—abuse that should have landed them in jail.

For years, Marjorie lived with the belief that her strong personality was sinful. She wrestled with who she was and wished she were quieter and more socially acceptable. She told me she used to cry to God, "Why can't I just be quiet like the pastor's wife?" A few years ago, a female friend who works in church leadership finally helped Marjorie to break free of the lie, "If you're strong, you're trying to be like a man." Nevertheless, even though she now feels internally free to embrace who she was created to be as a woman, she still believes that most men see her as being unsafe for Church leadership.

As a recognized and successful professional, Gina sits on the board of an influential organization within her field. Despite her achievements, she felt overlooked and ignored in her home church until just a few years ago, when she joined her husband on the church board. Though she had wanted to be on the church board for years and had gifts that would make her a valuable board member, her husband served on the board for more than a decade before she was invited to join him. Gina believes her promotion happened primarily because one of the pastors at her church—a man—strongly pushed for it.

Erin is one of the youngest women I interviewed, but she already walks in great influence and success as part of an itinerant ministry. Her comment on being a woman in the Church was, "It has been hard." Though no one told her this, experience taught her that if she wanted to have influence in the Church, she needed to marry a pastor or a worship leader. Then, in her early twenties, God spoke to her and changed her paradigm. She said, "At a time when many of my friends were getting married and having babies, I decided not to wait for a man to make my life happen. I let God direct my life, not a man." When she first started traveling, an older woman in ministry attacked Erin, telling her that she should not be in ministry because she wasn't married and didn't have a "covering." (Yes, it is a sad truth that many women are complicit in propping up the glass ceiling over other women in the Church.) Such resistance, though it didn't stop her, has been a regular aspect of her life in ministry.

Rebecca, who spent much of her career in subordinate positions within the Church, is now an executive-level leader both in her church and her community. The climb has been anything but easy. She told me of the time when she first realized she was gifted as a leader. Less than a decade ago, the staff at the church where she works took the DISC personality test. Her results revealed that she has a D-type (dominant) personality. Since that time, all of the women who tested as D-type personalities—except for her—have stopped working in the Church and have found their niche in the marketplace. The reality, Rebecca told me, was that there was no place for them to grow as leaders within the church. She, however, has stuck it out, and through her persistence, she is forging a path for many other women.

Sarah is an itinerant minister and author who has served on the staffs of multiple churches. After she and her husband received their ministry training at the same Bible college, they were jointly hired as associate pastors at a church. However, Sarah soon discovered that she was relegated to working with the women and children. When she realized this, something inside her died. She wrestled within herself: *Why am I disqualified? I have the exact same training as my husband.* After a year and a half in that environment, she had had enough; she decided to go back to school and get her degree in psychology so she could have the impact she wanted, even if it had to be outside the Church.

Not long after she started working on her degree, she began attending a new church where she was greatly impacted by the way everyone was validated. After several months there, Sarah went on a ministry trip led by the pastor. This pastor explained that he and his wife were both pastors, ministered equally together, and had equal say in all decisions. After hearing this, Sarah cried for an entire day. For the first time, she had met a man who really believed in and modeled honoring women as equals. A few months later, this same pastor invited Sarah to be on his church staff. This was especially significant because, at the time, her husband was not on staff there. For the first time, she felt validated as a person and a qualified leader, not just as "someone's wife." Receiving permission to be powerful from this pastor kept her from running to work in the secular world. She told me, "I never doubted that I was powerful, but I needed honor and value from men to give me the ability to have an impact, just like Jesus needed faith from the people to do miracles in His hometown."

Jamie, who is in her thirties, serves as a pastor of a local church alongside her husband after working for years as an educator. They are not the sole pastors of the church, but are part of a pastoral team that includes several married couples. As someone who did not grow up in the Church, Jamie's experience as a woman in leadership has been challenging. She grew up in a family where whoever was free would wash the dishes, be it mom or dad. Gender-specific labor roles didn't exist. But in the Church, she has found that gender-specific roles are deeply ingrained in many men, especially older men. Though they want to empower women, actually doing it requires a huge shift in their mindsets. Jamie believes this is why she has not felt validated or valued as a leader by the other men on her church's leadership team. She feels empowered by those under her authority, but her primary validation from her superiors comes because she's married to her husband and not because of who she is or what she brings to the table.

Helen is both an academic and a successful businesswoman who holds degrees in several disciplines, including a PhD in business. After spending years in corporate America, she now owns her own business and has authored a book. While she experienced restraints and limitations as a woman in the corporate world, Helen encountered far fewer difficulties there than she does when presenting her book and her ideas in the Christian world. On several occasions, when she looked for opportunities to present her book to business leaders in the Church, the church leaders directed her to the women's ministry. Her material is not oriented specifically toward women but toward businesspeople in general, yet these church leaders assumed that she would have nothing to offer the men.

Lack of Value for Personalities and Opinions

In the course of our conversations, I found that many of these women feel like their abilities are valued, but their *personalities* are not. Erin certainly feels that way. Her talents have promoted her into a position of influence over crowds of people. Yet within the day-to-day decision-making of the ministry where she works, she feels like her personality as a strong woman is not valued. In her experience, a strong personality is viewed as a negative in a woman, but a positive in a man.

She acknowledged that a lot is naturally required of her because of her calling, yet she has felt that even more has been required of her because of her gender. "Men aren't as trusting of a woman's capabilities, maturity, and intelligence," she noted, "so there have been more hoops I've had to jump through to prove myself." One of the biggest hoops involved her emotions. "I'm a very emotional woman," she admitted, "and I've had to work hard and learn how to keep my emotions in check." But as Erin has learned to control her emotions, she also noticed that the standards for men are lower in this area. Men generally assume that women are overly emotional and they (men) are not. This creates an environment in which there's more grace for emotional slips in men than in women. When her male co-workers express anger or discouragement, the other men typically respond with sympathy. Yet when Erin has slipped, she has been reprimanded for being "too emotional."

In general, Erin feels like her peers and superiors—all men—have wanted her to fit into a male mold of what makes a good leader. This wasn't intentional on their part; they were simply working from the only grid with which they were familiar. Erin finally pointed out this dynamic to her boss, and since then, he has changed the way he leads her. He has stopped trying to fit her into a male mold and has turned his focus toward helping her become a good leader *as a woman*. Erin is thankful for this, yet admits that they still have a long way to go toward making this a reality.

Similarly, Marjorie feels that her opinions have been very valued in the secular world by men and women and by her superiors, but they have not been valued in the Church. "I have never been in a secular job where I wasn't honored and where they weren't like, 'How can we clone you?' But I have never gotten that in the Church." Like Erin, Marjorie feels that the Church has valued her performance and achievement, but not her personality, which she has been told is "too strong" and "intimidating." When she was a little girl, her father, who was far from authoritarian, would often tell her, "You can do anything." Her experience in the Church has been a far cry from that promise.

Jamie echoed Marjorie's sentiments. While working in secular education, she always felt validated and confident as a communicator and leader. However, in the church where she pastors, she feels like her superiors don't even know her well enough to know what her abilities are, let alone value them. She is on the team primarily because of who she's married to. When she first began attending the church where she now pastors, one of the female leaders regularly talked about empowering women. At that time, Jamie thought, *Why are you still talking about this? I'm empowered.* But when she started working as a pastor, she began to understand why the woman spent so much time on the subject. She had not realized the glass ceiling was there until she smacked her head against it. She told me, "The closer you get to the top, the thinner the air becomes for women."

Once, when Rebecca suggested that her church invite a particular female speaker to minister there more often, she was told the woman was "too political and yells too much." At that time, several male speakers who exhibited these same characteristics were regular ministers at their church, but as Rebecca observed, "It was acceptable because it was a male package rather than a female one." Rebecca recognizes that this lack of value in many churches is not malicious. "It's just tradition—what people see all around them—and it's hard to break out of that mindset."

"The Church sometimes has an expectation of who I am as a woman that is not real, and that limits my influence," Sarah simply said. "Not all women are alike. They should be valued for their callings and not just categorized into one lump," she elaborated, citing the assumption in many churches that all women are good with children's ministry. "Jesus sees people by our identity and potential, which *isn't* defined by our race or gender." Gina agreed with Sarah, but said she, like many women, had learned to present herself in a culturally acceptable way, which essentially meant "toning down" her femininity in order to be effective in the male world. "You can get away with a lot as a woman if you're smart about it," she said. Sarah, however, wants a better solution: "We need to celebrate the differences between the genders without having to diminish one of them."

Working with Male Peers and Superiors

When I asked about her experience working with men, Marjorie told me that, though she has always been given very positive reviews by her coworkers and those she supervises, her male superior in the Church regularly tells her that she's not a good team builder. The only explanation she can find for this inconsistency is, once again, her strong personality, "I don't think I would have been corrected as much in regard to my personality if I was a man," she said. She wonders if her personality is the reason she has not been promoted.

As the first top-level female leader at her church (though she is not the senior pastor), Rebecca faced a great deal of resistance when being considered for the position. When she finally was hired, she was given limitations that her male peers were not. Many of the men who worked under her were paid more than she was. But after a year or two of seeing her prove her competence in her position, her male coworkers began advocating for greater equality on her behalf. Since then, many of the inequities have been resolved, and Rebecca feels accepted and supported as a leader in her church.

For Erin, the opportunity to work for spiritual fathers who believe in her, fight for her, and allow her to learn from their abilities and mistakes has been a highlight of working with men in the Church. However, her experience with many of her male coworkers has often left her feeling like an outsider. "I don't like being treated like 'one of the guys,'" she says. "I want respect, not rude joking and familiarity."

Erin told me a story about an attempt she made to help some of her coworkers reconcile their differences. She noticed that many of her male coworkers had a problem with one of the other men, but none of them wanted to talk to him about it. As the issue escalated, Erin decided to step up and confront this coworker even though she personally was not offended at him. She thought she could help solve the problem as a third party and restore peace to the office. However, when she talked to this man about it, he flippantly dismissed her, saying, "We're just men working." He was saying, "You don't understand because you're a woman. You're just overreacting." He absolutely refused to listen to her.

Erin couldn't believe it. To help him see that the issue she had brought up really was an issue, she called a meeting with the whole team. She explained the problem, and one by one, the other men confirmed that she had accurately represented their feelings. As the tension built in the room, Erin worked hard to mediate between her coworkers and keep a peaceful, rational atmosphere. She didn't want everyone to gang up and be too hard on him. But despite her efforts, it was clear he felt hurt. All of a sudden, he turned to her and said, "This would have never happened if it wasn't for you!" He blamed the whole thing on her. Worse, not one of the men in the room defended her. Erin chose to walk out of the confrontation and not defend herself. She knows that if she had reacted emotionally and talked to someone on the team the way that man had talked to her, she would have been confronted about it.

Like Erin, Jamie feels thankful for the chance to work with men of character who are good-hearted and emotionally and spiritually healthy. She trusts them and is challenged by their strengths. However, she says that overall the experience of working side-by-side with them has been hard. She feels she's perceived as being not "up to par" as a leader because she's a woman. "I feel like I'm the 'gap-filler,'" she told me. "I'm there to fill in the gaps they leave, and 80 percent of the time I feel like I'm seen as 'just the wife.'"

Jamie was sure to clarify that she loves being a wife and that she and her husband have a very close relationship, yet in her role at the church, she wishes she was appreciated as an individual, not simply as an appendage to her husband. "Only 20 percent of the time do I feel personally validated as a leader."

Gina simply said, "It has been difficult to be ignored for so many years."

The Inconsistencies

The existence of a glass ceiling means that there's a breakdown between what's being said and what's being done. This inconsistency manifests in a variety of ways. Elizabeth told me that when she travels for ministry, she is often asked, "Who are the powerful women of your church, and where are they?" In her experience, people are looking for churches that not only preach equality for men and women, but *obviously* demonstrate it by making room for qualified women to lead at every level of leadership—especially the senior, or most visible, level. Elizabeth has concluded that unless powerful women are allowed to be in a place of prominence as speakers and teachers, a church cannot advance in empowering their women.

Gina echoed her thoughts. "We talk about women in leadership, but we don't have many—at least not at the top levels and not speaking on

Sundays." This is important, she said, because women need to see other women in ministry in order to believe it's possible for them. They need role models.

Sarah also affirmed that without actually seeing female senior leaders in a church, it's hard to believe that, women can really be leaders there. She told me, "Little girls aren't saying, 'I want to be a pastor' because there's no model for that. Instead, the model women have is to be the wife of a powerful man. They're rarely taught the empowering message of the Word and to discover what God wants them to do—that anything is possible. Women, thus, gravitate toward a lower expectation and role in the Church."

Jamie sees acute inconsistencies in the ways she's treated compared with the way her husband is treated. Though they work as a team, she feels like her opinion is not even on the radar for their male superiors when it comes to making decisions. Her husband is invited to meetings and given actual authority, but she is not. Jamie said, "There's a difference between being 'liked' and being invited into meetings and intentionally groomed." In her experience, this grooming for leadership has primarily been reserved for young men, so much so that she admitted, "I have no clue how I would promote another woman into leadership at our church unless she is married to a male leader." Jamie told me that her husband is her biggest champion. He is listening to her concerns in this area, and she hopes that together the two of them can bring true change to the environment for women at their home church. There's equality on the lower levels of leadership in the church, Jamie told me, but noted that there's a definite cap to what women are invited into. "It makes me sick to see just men up there because I know that's not what God is like," she added.

"I hear a 'yes,' but don't see any action backing it up," said Erin. "It just seems like the men who want to empower women don't really know how to make it happen."

Rebecca gave one reason for this problem: "When the issue of women speaking or leading in the Church comes up, many men say, 'I haven't even studied it myself.'" They have culturally progressed—their wives aren't wearing head coverings—but they haven't taken the time to really find answers to the questions. "It's easier to just maintain how it is," she observed. "They don't feel the need for change—especially those leaders who are married to women who aren't advocating for it."

Living Voiceless

Voicelessness, a buzz word among feminists and minority groups, can be defined as being "without the power or right to express an opinion."[3] When I asked whether she had ever felt voiceless, Erin quickly answered, "All the time!" She told me she constantly voices her opinions, but feels like she's not heard. Sometimes she does get an affirmative response, but often it is not followed by action. Because Erin is a well-known stage personality, she has, by default, a voice within her organization, yet she told me, "It feels more like they're trying to appease me because they have to rather than truly valuing my intelligence and discernment."

Similarly, Sarah told me that many times she has felt like her opinion was not important and that she was not looked to for her position on a matter. She felt categorized. "It was assumed I wouldn't have an answer," she told me.

Though now she holds a position in which she has more of a voice, Rebecca told me that for years she had to talk through her husband because, on her own, she would not have been taken seriously. Recently, a friend of hers, who is very successful in business, told Rebecca, "When you talk [about your work in the Church], it sounds like you're in politics,"—referring to the intensity of the environment and the criticism she sometimes faces as a woman.

With pain in her eyes, Marjorie told me that she has often felt voiceless. Again and again, she has had to force her opinion forward because there's no graceful way for her to be heard, and then deal with criticism for asserting herself. She's often been told she's too aggressive. "Pursuit is seen as a negative in women," she commented, "but as a positive in men." For this reason, she believes many women have difficulty pursuing their dreams and making their voices heard. They find fault with themselves instead. When they're not promoted, they simply accept it as "not God's timing" rather than going after their destiny in the way men do.

Jamie and her husband often have the opportunity to meet with church and ministry leaders from around the world. In about 90 percent of these encounters, she estimates, these leaders, who are usually men, talk primarily to her husband and not to her. They tell him all about what they're doing and ask to hear about his work, but they don't even think to engage Jamie in the conversation. They often encourage her husband with a word about how he's called as a leader and how God wants to use him—which is all true—but they completely leave Jamie out of it, even though the two of them minister together as a couple. "Being so overlooked is a painful experience," Jamie said. It's like she's invisible and has nothing of value to offer to a conversation or an organization.

Pressure to Conform to Roles and Places

Elizabeth, who is happily married to a top-level staff member at her church, has faced pressure for the way that her marriage does not fit traditional ideas of male and female roles. When Elizabeth travels for ministry, which she does much more than her husband, her husband is regularly asked where his wife is, as though it's not acceptable for her to be traveling if he is not. Her husband has had to learn how to answer this question without feeling threatened or diminished. Reflecting on this, Elizabeth commented that it takes a very secure, honoring spouse to allow his wife to become a powerful force within the Church.

While Sarah was in Bible College, she asked one of the professor's wives if she would disciple her. In response, this woman began to share her belief that a woman should lay down her personal dreams in order to support her husband's vocation. Sarah knew instantly that this woman would not be a good mentor for her, so she moved on. She decided to never again open up her heart and her dreams to other women in the Church who might put her down for having them, "I made a promise to myself at that time that, if I got the chance. I would disciple women to fulfill their call and never make them feel as I had been made to feel—like a second-class citizen."

Marjorie noticed a significant difference in the way that men talk to women in both secular and Christian environments. While working at a Christian institution, a female coworker came to her for advice because a man had said to her, "Wow, you're emotional. Are you on your period?" Marjorie said that never in any of the secular places where she worked had she heard of a man speaking so disrespectfully to a woman. But sadly, as she learned, this sort of offensive behavior is not uncommon in the Christian sphere.

Rebecca had many stories of receiving seemingly insignificant comments designed to "put her in her place" and communicate her second-class status as a woman in the Church. On more than one occasion, she has sat on an airplane beside a Christian man who asked her, "What do you do?" After she responded, "My husband and I are in ministry together," the man would correct her, saying something like, "You mean, your husband is a minister, right?"

Other comments have been less subtle. When travelling to speak at churches, Rebecca has had men approach her with open Bibles, quoting Scripture to support their belief that she should not be teaching in the church. Someone once told her to "soften her eyes" while she speaks in order to seem more "feminine." On one occasion, a man walked into the building where she was working. Though she was not the only person in the room, this man approached her and said, "You look like someone's secretary. Maybe you can help me." Several years ago, she sat in a staff meeting at her church in which the pastor informed all the staff that the women would not be getting paid as much as the men because the women were not the "bread-winners" for their families. She cried for days after that meeting.

Rebecca also told me of a class for young women that she sometimes teaches. In it, she asks the women what their dreams are. A large percentage say, "To be a wife and mother." To that, Rebecca responds, "Okay, that's going to happen soon, and then what?" She asks, "What do you want to do after that?" Again and again, the young women who take this class are completely stunned. They have no idea what to say. In the Church, they've been taught that marriage and motherhood are all they can do. Instead, Rebecca tells them to go for their dreams. She says, "I believe women *can* have it all, though maybe not all at once."

Why Should We Care?

Each of these women has painful stories about crashing into the Church's glass ceiling. Some have found healing in their hearts. Others are still hurting. But all of them are proof for us that this ceiling really does exist. They are evidence that it is still harder than we think for a woman to "happen," even in the freest of churches.

If we are willing to hear it, these stories are an invitation for us to stand up and fight for liberty and truth. Many of us have spent a long time being comfortable because we couldn't hear or understand the truth about what it feels like to be a woman in the Church. Now we have heard a small piece of the female story—a piece that comes from women who are considered, by many, to already be powerful. They are mature, intelligent, and competent women, and for the most part, they work in and attend churches that believe in gender equality. The oppression of women in the Church is not a significant theme in their lives or ministries, and they are not the sort of women who spend a lot of time complaining about how men have victimized them. They are determined to overcome the hurdles to their destinies—no matter the form they take.

Yet they refuse to deny the limitations they've experienced.

Their stories expose a shameful reality that we must examine. A problem cannot be solved if we don't realize it exists. Hopefully you are beginning to see this problem is real. The good news is that Heaven has both the courage and the answer we need. The question is: What will we do with what we have heard?

One thing we must do is to stop using the Bible to excuse the glass ceiling. It's time for us to take a closer look at some of those controversial verses about women in the Church and make sure we're not allowing surface readings of them to create complacency about cultivating a high value for what woman have to bring to the table.

Chapter Four

PAUL: APOSTLE OF FREEDOM AND EQUALITY

I have asked many male church leaders if they have ever studied the issue of women leading in the Church. The typical answer I receive is, "No, I have not studied it for myself."

Essentially, these men are telling me that they are comfortable with the status quo and are unmotivated to change—a common attitude among men at the top. Unfortunately, they are unaware that maintaining this comfortable position is hazardous. Comfortable people risk becoming stagnant and mediocre, because they avoid opportunities to grow and learn. They also risk being out of touch with reality, because they usually surround themselves with other comfortable people and avoid "perspective diversity."

I believe the Church has invited both of these hazards by failing to proactively pursue God's place for women in church leadership. Powerful women create vital opportunities for growth and bring needed viewpoints to leadership in the Body. Dismissing these opportunities and perspectives is foolish.

But there is another danger to maintaining the comfortable male-dominant status quo. It is not fun to talk about, but it must be done. This is the danger of being complacent about the very real abuse that is directed at women in the Church.

For many years in my career as a social worker, I worked with groups of men who had been convicted of domestic violence. I spent up to two years with some of them. They were absolutely clueless as to why violence was such a pattern in their lives. It was my job to confront them with the truth that many men, though they don't like to admit it, harbor an inner fear and hatred of women. This is known as *misogyny*. Misogyny is still prevalent today, thanks to the patriarchal paradigm. When men believe, or want to believe, that women are "naturally" subordinate—as many men do—they view them as inferior in value. When you view people as inferior in value, you will mistreat them through neglect or through active abuse.

Spousal abuse is just as common in evangelical churches as it is anywhere else. Approximately twenty-five percent of Christian homes experience abuse of some kind. One study asked six thousand pastors what they would do if a woman came to them for counsel about domestic abuse. Here are the shocking results:

- Twenty-six percent would counsel the wife to continue to submit to her husband, no matter what.

- Twenty-five percent would tell the wife the abuse was her own fault for failing to submit in the first place.

- Fifty percent said that women should be willing to "tolerate some level of violence" because it is better than divorce.[1]

These statistics are hard to believe, but they point to a reality we can't ig¬nore. Many men—Christian men—abuse their wives physically, sexually, or emotionally, and often the Church provides little protection for these women. And while many of us may know instinctively that this is not okay, we have difficulty confronting it because the idea of male superiority is ingrained in our psyches—ingrained even more thoroughly because we have used the Bible to ratify it.

Actively Pursuing Truth

I recently saw an interview with a Muslim cleric, who was explaining what the Koran taught about the role of a man in the home:

Allah said in the Koran that men are guardians of women because

Allah has made one superior to the other and because they support them with their means. So men have guardianship over women, but this does not mean that they can oppress or humiliate their wives. Any group of people must have a leader. A state must have a leader, a king, a president, an emir, an oman. The same is true for government; ministries must have a minister in charge, and departments must have directors. This is human nature; there must be leadership. The household consists of several family members who must have a leader. Who is the leader? The man. No one can claim the verse "men are the guardians of women" shows contempt for women. This is not true. The husband is the leader of the family, and he runs its affairs. He is in charge of the family; he is the shepherd of his family. He is responsible for his flock, as the prophet said. A man is a shepherd to his household and is responsible for them. So the man is the guardian. He must act justly; he must raise his children well. He must fulfill his obligations towards his wife and children. As for the woman, she cannot leave the house without her husband's permission, just like no employee can leave the office without permission from the boss.[2]

As I watched this interview, I was struck by how familiar it felt to hear such patriarchal logic explained and justified by religious texts. I could easily imagine certain Bible-thumpers saying "amen" to this cleric on one or two points. Though they may not necessarily conclude that wives should be prohibited from leaving the house without permission, many in the Church still read and teach certain parts of the Bible in a way very similar, even nearly identical, to the way this Muslim cleric reads the Koran. For example, people teach that Paul's statement, *"the head of woman is man"* (1 Cor. 11:3), clearly means that women are subordinate to men. Likewise, the passage in 1 Peter 3 is often interpreted to mean that a woman must do whatever her husband says and that being "weaker vessels" means that women are less capable than men:

Wives, likewise, be submissive to your own husbands...For in this manner, in former times, the holy women who trusted in God also adorned themselves, being submissive to their own husbands, as Sarah obeyed Abraham, calling him lord, whose daughters you are if you do good and are not afraid with any terror. Husbands, likewise, dwell with them with understanding, giving honor to the wife, as to the weaker vessel, and as being heirs together of the grace of life, that your prayers may not be hindered. (1 Pet. 3:1, 5-7)

Then, of course, there are Paul's comments on women speaking in church. These are still used to authorize teaching that women have nothing of real value to contribute and should never hold a leadership role in the Church:

And I do not permit a woman to teach or to have authority over a man, but to be in silence. (1 Tim. 2:12)

And if they want to learn something, let them ask their own husbands at home; for it is shameful for women to speak in church. (1 Cor. 14:35)

These teachings have been around for a long time. They form one thread in a longstanding religious tradition of using the Bible to prop up the patriarchal paradigm and its institutions—a tradition that has always been at war with the real Gospel.

One of the great battles in this ongoing war, the battle over the issue of slavery, reached its climax in our nation 150 years ago. In the years leading up to the Civil War, slavery in America was ardently defended by teachers who quoted Scripture to make their case that this institution was a God-ordained, "natural" social reality. They pointed out that Abraham, the Father of Faith, owned slaves, that when one of Abraham's wife Sarah's slaves escaped, God told her to return to her mistress (see Gen. 16), and that Isaac and Jacob also had many male and female slaves. Even one of the Ten Commandments says, *"You shall not covet your neighbor's house; you shall not covet your neighbor's wife, nor his male servant, nor his female servant, nor his ox, nor his donkey, nor anything that is your neighbor's"* (Exod. 20:17). And, like the teachers of female submission, the pro-slavery Bible teachers also claimed that the apostle Paul was on their side, seeing that he wrote on several occasions about the submission of slaves:

Slaves, be obedient to those who are your masters according to the flesh, with fear and trembling, in the sincerity of your heart, as to Christ... (Eph. 6:5 NASB)

Slaves, in all things obey those who are your masters on earth, not with external service, as those who merely please men, but with sincerity of heart, fearing the Lord. (Col. 3:22 NASB)

All who are under the yoke as slaves are to regard their own masters as worthy of all honor so that the name of God and our doctrine will not be spoken against. (1 Tim. 6:1 NASB)

On the other side of the battle, abolitionists were also preaching the Bible, arguing that the pro-slavery camp was not just off-base, but dead wrong in their use of the Scriptures. Slavery, said the abolitionists, absolutely contradicted the Gospel. The real Gospel did not affirm the old "natural" oppressive human institutions; it drew people into a new social reality, *"Where there is neither Greek nor Jew, circumcised nor uncircumcised, barbarian, Scythian, slave nor free"* (Col. 3:11). The real Gospel set the captives "free at last!"

We know who won the slavery argument (and, it must never be forgotten, at what cost). We know who was reading the Bible correctly and who was not. And abolition is not the only example of social and moral progress in our history fueled by the Gospel; a little research into the movements for civil rights, child labor laws, education, and women's suffrage will reveal that they all trace back in significant ways to its truths. The Bible is the source of the very ideals of freedom and equality upon which our nation was founded.

Yet the war for truth rages on today. People aren't using the Bible to defend slavery anymore, but they are still using it to encourage ideas that resonate with Islam and other patriarchal religions. Thus, as in every generation, there is a pressing need for Bible teachers to equip believers with the ability to "rightly divide the word of truth" (see 2 Tim. 2:15) so they won't fall into the bad habit of using the Bible to defend the traditions of man against the Gospel.

We must understand that the Bible is full of statements that can be, and have been, used to support two *absolutely contradictory* positions. The Bible has all the freedom in it that we could ever want—it's packed with freedom. But it also has plenty of slavery, genocide, and dysfunction. The question we need to ask is, "What are we looking for in the Bible?" We will find what we are looking for, and our search is always defined by the attitude of our hearts. If our hearts are driven by fear, then we will find the patriarchal paradigm. We will find verses that excuse or validate slavery, racism, sexism, segregation, retaliation, ostracism, and domination. But if our hearts are driven by humility and a hunger for God, we will find the Kingdom. We will find truths that set the captives free, raise the oppressed, equally honor men and women, and destroy every kind of segregation through the unity of the Spirit.

I am not saying that we can cherry-pick verses from the Bible. Picking and choosing is exactly the problem with people who read the Bible from a patriarchal paradigm. The Bible's overarching message is firmly anti-patriarchal. You have to cut and twist a whole lot more of it to support oppression than you do to study and resolve its paradoxes to support Kingdom freedom. Nevertheless, people who teach the Kingdom but avoid addressing controversial passages like those above weaken their biblical integrity and do nothing to stop the chronic, generational problem of men who use them to oppress women.

Paul's Blueprint for Freedom

Jesus' treatment of women was pretty much void of anything resembling patriarchy. People have a hard time mining the words and acts of Jesus in order to justify a belief in female inferiority. The authority they look to instead is Paul. And Paul made some very controversial statements about women and their role in both church and marriage.

But think about it: Would Jesus, the champion of women, allow a patriarchal apostle to pen most of the New Testament?

Yeah, that doesn't make sense to me either.

So an important question to keep in mind is, "How is Paul's teaching on women in line with what Jesus taught and practiced?"

We also need to look for consistency between Paul's controversial verses and the rest of his teaching. This is anything but straightforward. What does it mean that the man who wrote, *"I do not permit a woman to teach or to have authority over a man..."* also wrote, *"There is neither Jew nor Greek, there is neither slave nor free, there is neither male nor female; for you are all one in Christ Jesus?"* (Gal. 3:28)

We can only understand and resolve the surface contradictions in such statements by understanding Paul's heart and the primary message of his ministry by digging deeper into the historical and textual context.

Paul stood at the forefront of the biggest cultural transformation in human history as an apostolic architect. He was commissioned to establish the blueprint of Heaven's justice and freedom on earth. His mission was to preach the Gospel to the Gentiles and to lay the foundation for a new Kingdom culture where Jews and Gentiles could unite around a common identity, common core values, and a common relationship with God. But, this would prove harder than it sounds. Both Jews and Gentiles came to Christianity with problematic cultural traditions and beliefs directly out of line with the Gospel.

Among the Jews, Paul fought a sustained battle to prove that Christianity was an entirely New Covenant—a new relationship between God and humanity—that superseded the Old Covenant. The Jews never imagined that the Messiah's ministry would be directed toward anyone except them, God's chosen people. It was a major stretch for Jewish Christians to realize that God wanted to give *everyone* else the same status, especially without making them Jews. For centuries, the only way a Gentile could enter into covenant with God was to convert to Judaism. This is why many "Judaizers" traveled around Palestine teaching new converts that they needed not only to be baptized, but to be circumcised and to practice the Law. Paul went to great lengths to show that these cultural demands amounted to going back to the Old Covenant.

Paul struck at the very heart of Jewish identity by preaching against circumcision, confronting the deep-seated beliefs in their cultural and spiritual superiority, privilege, and authority that had sustained the legacy of Jewish racism toward Gentiles. As a former zealous Pharisee and Law expert, he was probably the only one who could have gotten away with it. Even Peter caved into the Judaizers at one point (see Gal. 2:11-13). But Paul carried such a deep and thorough knowledge of the differences between the Old and New Covenants (and had crossed so fully into the New) that he couldn't be swayed.

Circumcision, the sign of the Old Covenant, was exclusive to Jewish men. Baptism was all-inclusive. You didn't need the same equipment for baptism as you did for circumcision. You just needed to be able to get wet.

Baptism was a clear signpost that the legitimizing path of obedience, faith, and righteousness was no longer limited to men. This gave women in particular a value they had never had. In the Jewish culture, women only gained social value and spiritual legitimacy through marriage to a circumcised man and through giving birth to male children who could be circumcised. But in his stand against the requirement of circumcision, Paul was saying, "No more thinking like that! There are no more Jews and Gentiles, no more slaves, and no more male and female value systems. It has been done away with in Christ. Now we all have the same value!"

On the Gentile side of the fence, Paul had different cultural value systems to confront. This is primarily where his comments about women in church in 1 Corinthians and 1 Timothy (the comments that have been used to limit or disqualify women from ministry) come into play.

I want to look at two of these phrases and show you just how off it is to read them at face value and then use them to cap women in ministry. Then, in the next chapter, we'll dig into Paul's teaching on "headship" in marriage. Our beliefs about gendered authority in the Church and gendered authority in marriage are all connected. And we need to cover what Paul teaches about both in order to develop a solid biblical understanding of what authority and gender mean in a Kingdom context.

Specific Women, Not All Women

Paul's letters to the Corinthian church and to Timothy, a pastor in Ephesus, are letters of guidance for handling various problems that arose largely from the pagan Gentile cultures of these cities. As personal letters to *specific* people in *specific* places, they reference previous correspondence and personal history that failed to make it into any accessible records. Bible scholars and historians attempt to make educated guesses as to what Paul meant in these letters, because a face-value reading is clearly out of line with the rest of what Paul (and Jesus) taught and practiced.

We'll start with Paul's comments in 1 Corinthians. Paul wrote this letter to the Corinthian church, which he originally planted and oversaw for two years with a ministry team that included Aquila, Silas, Timothy, and *Priscilla* (see Acts 18:1-5,11). That's right, a woman, Priscilla—who

later trained Apollos and went on to lead churches with her husband in
Ephesus and Rome (see Acts 18:24-26, Rom. 16:3-5)—was one of Paul's
core leaders while he was in Corinth. Scholars also believe that one of the
Corinthian house churches was led by a woman named Chloe.[4] At the end
of Romans, Paul mentions another female church leader connected with
Corinth, Phoebe, who he refers to as a deacon or minister (Gr. *diakonos*)
and commends to the Roman church, urging them to receive her ministry.[5]

The presence of women church leaders partnering with Paul in Corinth
and throughout his ministry (Paul mentions at least ten female ministry
colleagues in his letters[6]) suggests that nothing he wrote was intended to
prohibit women in leadership, including those troublesome verses in 1
Corinthians 14:

> *Let your women keep silent in the churches, for they are not permitted to speak;*
> *but they are to be submissive, as the law also says. And if they want to learn*
> *something, let them ask their own husbands at home; for it is shameful for*
> *women to speak in church.* (1 Cor. 14:34-35 NIV)

This passage is very hard for most women to read.

And it should be, because it was *not* written to "most" women.

It was written to "your" women. Or *specific* women in the Corinthian
church.

Paul was not affirming a universal "shut up" to all women in the Church.
After all, in this same letter, Paul referred positively to women praying and
prophesying in church meetings, which definitely included speaking (see 1
Cor. 11:5).

Paul was addressing disorder apparently involved certain women who
were constantly speaking up and disrupting the service and the presentation
of the Gospel (see 1 Cor. 14:23-25). Paul was not dealing with the fact that
they were speaking, but that they were keeping unbelievers who might
attend the meetings from hearing a clear message.[7]

Many scholars strongly believe that 1 Corinthians 14:34-35 *are not even*
Paul's words.

The first clue is the phrase *"as the law also says."* This is clearly not referring
to the Old Testament, but to the Jewish oral law, the Talmud. Paul, like
Jesus before him, was not known for preaching the Talmud. He was
known for showing how the Gospel cut through the traditions of man and

superseded the Old Covenant. He was known for *vehemently* emphasizing that we weren't to go back to the Law.

It would be very strange for Paul to blatantly contradict Jesus' model of totally rejecting the Jewish cultural prohibition against women speaking in religious meetings.

It would also be very strange for Paul to blatantly contradict what he had just said two verses earlier: *"You can **all** prophesy one by one..."* (1 Cor. 14:31).

Imagine sitting in a class and hearing the teacher announce: "Hey, I want *everyone* in the room to tell the class about their summer vacation. One person at a time. And also, all the girls can't talk."

Yeah, that doesn't make sense. It's actually crazy.

Believing that Paul meant both statements to be authoritative shoots his credibility in the head. This is the second clue.

A third clue is the presence of a Greek symbol (η) Paul used repeatedly throughout 1 Corinthians. Scholars assign two basic meanings to this sign. The first meaning is that it indicates that Paul just quoted from another source—most likely from the previous letter he had received from the Corinthian church (referenced in 1 Cor. 7:1) explaining the problems that had been going on requesting Paul's guidance.[8]

If this is true, then what we are reading in these verses about women keeping silent in church is actually the policy certain people in the Corinthian church—obviously Judaizers—had thought to implement for dealing with their disruptive women. They were saying, "We know how to deal with these ladies who keep interrupting the meetings. We'll just fall back on the old rule about women not speaking at all in the synagogue and only learning from their husbands at home."

The second meaning of this Greek symbol is that it is an "expletive of disassociation."[9] If it was used in that sense, then Paul is reacting strongly *against* the words he has just quoted. David Hamilton writes, "The closest equivalent to (η) in English would be 'What?' or 'Nonsense!' or 'No way!'"[10] Significantly, Paul uses this expletive *twice* in the 1 Corinthians 14:36—the only verse where he does so. Here's a possible translation of this passage:

> *"Let your women keep silent in the churches, for they are not permitted to speak; but they are to be submissive, as the law also says. And if they want to*

learn something, let them ask their own husbands at home; for it is shameful for women to speak in church."

(η) Nonsense! Did the word of God originate with you? Or (η) what? Are you the only ones it has reached? (1 Cor. 14:36)

Paul was *passionately disagreeing* with the Corinthians's law-based solution to their disruptive women by reminding them that the Gospel had come to all people by God's choice, and that they were not to go back to the old patriarchal system of controlling who could or could not have access to the truth.

Understanding that Paul is dialoguing with the Corinthians in this passage finally makes these verses actually sound like Paul. It allows us to recognize the voice of the apostle who truly was a champion for freedom and equality. It allows us to hear the heart of the former Pharisee who fought to emphasize to Jews and Gentiles alike that in the New Covenant, *no one is disqualified.* The fact that we have mistakenly used what we thought were Paul's words (but weren't) to shut women up in the Church has to be one of the greatest tragedies in history.

It's time to preach Paul's real words and show the world that God has called and qualified everyone—men and women—to proclaim His word.

Usurping Authority, Not Having Authority

Now, let's look at one of Paul's most difficult passages on women, 1 Timothy 2:11-15:

Let a woman learn in silence with all submission. And I do not permit a woman to teach or to have authority over a man, but to be in silence. For Adam was formed first, then Eve. And Adam was not deceived, but the woman being deceived, fell into transgression. Nevertheless she will be saved in childbearing if they continue in faith, love, and holiness, with self-control.

The primary issue Paul addressed in this letter to Timothy was false teaching that had been infiltrating the Ephesian church, some of which had been coming through certain women (see 1 Tim. 1:3-4; 4:1,7; 5:13).[11] According to Bible scholars, Gnostic heresies were circulating through that region at that time and tempting new believers away from the pure

Gospel.[12] Ephesus was also home to the temple of Artemis, and many under Timothy's leadership had undoubtedly been saved out of this cult, but were still vulnerable to its influence.

Some women, probably illiterate, began spreading strange doctrines— *"…saying things which they ought not"* (1 Tim. 5:13). They were claiming to be teachers of the law. Some even spread a heretical belief that Eve was created before Adam and that she had freed the world by listening to the serpent.[13]

In verse 12, Paul commanded that these women must not teach their heresies or seek to dominate men, but instead should be quiet and listen. In verses 13 and 14, Paul opposed the idea that women are superior to men, which is what these women were teaching.

However, it does *not* follow that he was claiming that men are superior to women.[14] As we already noted, Paul believed that neither male nor female were superior, but that all are one in Christ.

Paul's final comment, in verse 15, seems at first glance to suggest that women are saved through having children, which obviously contradicts the Gospel of salvation through faith and sends us in search of the back story. Women in Ephesus commonly prayed to Artemis so that they would be saved through childbirth. In fact, one of the alternative names for Artemis was Soteira, which derives from the Greek word for salvation, *soterias*. Thus, many scholars believe Paul was exhorting women to put their trust in Christ for salvation during childbearing rather than trusting in Artemis.[15] According to this interpretation, verse 15, like the two verses before it, confronts areas of syncretism in the Ephesian church, where the teachings of the Artemis cult were causing some to depart from the faith (see 1 Tim. 4:1).

The word *authority* (*authentein* in the Greek) in verse 12—*"I do not permit a woman…to have authority over a man"*—is not used anywhere else in the Bible. Most often "authority" is translated from the word *exousia*. Unlike *exousia*, which speaks of rightful or positive authority, *authentein*, writes J. Lee Grady, "has a forceful and extremely negative connotation. It implies a more specific meaning than 'to have authority over' and can be translated 'to dominate,' 'to usurp,' or 'to take control.'"[16] The noun form of this word can be defined as "one who with his own hands kills another or himself."[17]

Paul was obviously *not* saying that women could not have authority or teach in general, but that these particular women (or any person, for that matter) must not violently dominate or usurp authority. Further support for this point exists in the fact that in his second letter to Timothy, Paul honors Timothy's mother and grandmother, Lois and Eunice, for passing their faith on to Timothy (see 2 Tim. 1:5). Timothy learned the Gospel from women, so it's doubtful that he or Paul would prohibit *all* women from teaching or prohibit men from sitting under a woman's authority as a teacher.

As I said, this brief introduction to some of the work scholars have done to interpret these two tough passages is just that, an introduction. I trust it is enough for you to see that using these verses to disqualify women in leadership and ministry is weak and unwarranted. Yet sadly, it seems that in much of the Body of Christ, the religious traditions of the Judaizers continue to carry more weight in our beliefs about gender authority than the real-life examples of Paul and Jesus.

Unity Requires Equality

I recently read the famous story of the time when Anne Graham Lotz, Billy Graham's daughter, spoke at a pastor's convention. As she began, many of the men picked up their chairs and turned their backs to her. Though they were friends and supporters of her father, they refused to sit under her teaching because their traditions taught them that women cannot teach men in the Church.[18]

I do not believe that Paul or any of the apostles would approve of us using their teachings to perpetuate any belief that preserves this kind of disunity and dishonor in the Body of Christ. Paul taught that the clearest sign we are walking worthy of our calling and entering into the Kingdom is that we express the *"unity of the faith"* or the *"unity of the Spirit"* (Eph. 4:3,13). The very nature of unity is that it requires everyone involved to be free and powerful, and to have equal value.

For this reason, men and women will never find true unity or oneness as long as women are defined as "less" than men.

Many of us understand that God wants unity between men and women—particularly in marriage. In marriage, two become *one*. But there is a more general sense in which God designed men and women to be one in Christ. Sin violated this design and made us competitors instead of teammates.

But when Jesus died on the cross, He took the whole mass of alienated men and women and on that Day of Atonement—"at-one-ment"—He brought all of us together. *All* of us.

We are now members of one Body, called to participate in the perfect fellowship shared between the Father, Son, and Holy Spirit. That is Heaven's blueprint.

We see Heaven's blueprint clearly expressed in Acts 1, when, for the first time since the Garden of Eden, men and women came together in oneness: *"These all continued with* **one accord** *in prayer and supplication, with* **the women** *and Mary the mother of Jesus, and with His brothers"* (Acts 1:14). This group of men and women in "one accord" created an invitation for Heaven. We know what happened next. On the day of Pentecost, when *"they were all with* **one accord** *in one place"* (Acts 2:1), the Holy Spirit came upon them—all of them—*"and they were* **all** *filled with the Holy Spirit and began to speak with other tongues, as the Spirit gave them utterance"* (Acts 2:4).

The Holy Spirit didn't just bounce around to the men and skip over the women. He filled them all! As Peter explained to the onlookers, this outpouring was God's fulfillment of Joel 2:28-29:

> *I will pour out My Spirit on all flesh; your sons and* **your daughters** *shall prophesy, your old men shall dream dreams, your young men shall see visions. And also on My menservants and on My* **maidservants** *I will pour out My Spirit in those days.*

This is such a clear expression of God's intention for humanity. This is why a defining mark of revival is that as the Spirit increases, divisions decrease. Gender divisions, race divisions, and socio-economic divisions fade away as everyone encounters God together. As Heaven invades earth, Heaven's value system neutralizes prejudices and the effects of the patriarchal paradigm. That's why a black man, William Seymour, led the Azusa Street Revival in the racially segregated United States. That's why women like Maria Woodworth-Etter, Aimee Semple McPherson, and

Kathryn Kuhlman became leaders of revival during a time when women were never ordained or even considered for leadership.

Jesus provided the at-one-ment to bring us all back together, but many of us just can't seem to stop separating. Heaven's blueprint is simple enough, but living it has proven difficult. We have centuries of momentum to justify our urge to divide. It is time for a paradigm shift. It is time for us to decide, once and for all, that a second-class position cannot exist in the Church.

I'm not saying that we should disempower the men in order to empower women.

I am saying that we must learn to share our power and freedom as members of one Body.

This is what Christ modeled and prayed for, what Paul preached, and what we deeply long for as sons and daughters of God.

Chapter Five

THE HEAD AND THE HELPER

A successful businessman came home one day to find his wife in a tie-dyed cotton dress. She was a bit of a flower child, and she had purchased this new dress on a recent trip to San Francisco. Her husband was more of a redneck than a flower child, and he did not want "a hippy" in his house. He told his wife to take off the dress.

"No," she said. "I like it."

"Take it off or I will," he threatened her.

"You wouldn't dare," she said.

But he would, and he did. He grabbed her and stripped off the dress. She must have been planning to wear it only around the house, because she had nothing on underneath.

Then the husband threw her outside, because he could. He was bigger and stronger. He was the man, and he was the boss. The poor woman had to run to a neighbor's house to get some help.

It wasn't long before the husband found himself in my office, though not before he'd first spent some time in jail. I worked with domestic violence offenders for several years. As part of a diversion program, these men could choose to spend two and a half hours a week for a year counseling with me rather than going to jail for a year. In a little over five years, we put approximately 200 men through our program. In that time, I heard quite a few outrageous stories, but this one beat them all.

His actions were an extreme manifestation of the patriarchal paradigm (at least in America today—much worse happens around the world, and is considered a cultural norm in some places), but they illustrate the beliefs many of us have about what it means to be a man and to have authority over a woman.

Okay, we wouldn't throw our wives out naked on the curb, but if we're honest, many of us can relate to that inner fear of losing control— "Don't you dare defy me! I will make you pay for not respecting me as a man." A belief in male dominance feeds our fear of powerlessness and insignificance. It causes us to protect at all costs the system that says, "I'm big, you're little. I'm strong, you're weak. I'm rich, you're poor. Too bad." When it comes to men and women, or more specifically, husband and wife, insecure men like to think that only one person in the relationship gets to have a brain.

Parts of One Body

The patriarchal paradigm, driven by fear and self-protection, sees separation and opposition as the fundamental nature of relationships. It is an "every man for himself" attitude. But the Kingdom, once again, brings unity to our relationships—*"you **are all** one in Christ Jesus."* And out of that unity flows mutual interest in one another, equality, and cooperation. One of the most powerful biblical metaphors for the reality of this oneness is the Body of Christ: *"So we, being many, are one body in Christ, and individually members of one another"* (Rom. 12:5). We are all part of a whole that must flow together in order to stay alive, even though we each have a different function. This was God's original design at creation, and He has restored it through Jesus. We don't have to be afraid of each other anymore. We aren't on opposing sides. We are a team, a unit. We are designed to live together without fear.

Learning to think as members of a single body means learning to value people we wouldn't naturally value because we realize that we are connected and we need one another. Paul explains:

> *...no matter how significant you are, it is only because of what you are a part of. An enormous eye or a gigantic hand wouldn't be a body, but a monster. What we have is one body with many parts, each its proper size and in its proper place. No part is important on its own. Can you imagine Eye telling Hand, "Get lost; I don't need you"? Or, Head telling Foot, "You're fired; your*

job has been phased out"? As a matter of fact, in practice it works the other way—the "lower" the part, the more basic, and therefore necessary. You can live without an eye, for instance, but not without a stomach. When it's a part of your own body you are concerned with, it makes no difference whether the part is visible or clothed, higher or lower. You give it dignity and honor just as it is, without comparisons. If anything, you have more concern for the lower parts than the higher. If you had to choose, wouldn't you prefer good digestion to full-bodied hair? (1 Cor. 12:19-24 MSG)

The patriarchal paradigm cannot survive when you're thinking like a body part because unity undermines the "every man for himself" attitude. Furthermore, it turns the old strong/weak value system on its head. In our physical bodies, many of our most important parts are hidden and seemingly weak. A body builder is impressively strong, and his muscles are on display for all to see, but his muscles are not his most important part. He could survive a loss of muscle mass or even total paralysis. Take out his heart and we have another story. It is the internal, hidden organs that are referred to as *vital organs*. And of course, *all* the organs are needed for a healthy body. We don't pick and choose them from a buffet. If we don't have all of our organs, then we are disabled or diseased in some way. Likewise, if we aren't allowing all the parts of Christ's Body to function as they should, the Church will end up unhealthy, crippled, or even lifeless.

In the Kingdom, weakness is not a bad thing. In fact, as Jesus told Paul, weakness is exactly where God likes to show up and show off (see 2 Cor. 12:9). But in the patriarchal paradigm, weakness is bad. This is why men often read their negative associations with weakness into Peter's description of women as "the weaker vessel."

Husbands, likewise, dwell with them [your wives] *with understanding, giving honor to the wife, as to the weaker vessel, and as being heirs together of the grace of life, that your prayers may not be hindered.* (1 Pet. 3:7)

Believe it or not, Peter was actually contradicting the patriarchal paradigm by saying that women's physical weakness is a call for greater honor and regard! And just in case the men didn't understand him, he kept going. First, he reminded the men that their wives are equal heirs of salvation. Then he announced that if they continued to live out this patriarchal nonsense, God wouldn't answer their prayers. Those are strong words—about as strong as strong gets.

God wants us to know that there is a crippling effect when the Church is missing some of its parts. He values oneness. God is not okay with us putting down other members of His Body, all of whom He has called and equipped in different ways to carry His Spirit and His Gospel. As Paul put it, *"Who are you to judge another's servant? To his own master he stands or falls. Indeed, he will be made to stand, for God is able to make him stand"* (Rom. 14:4). Who are we to take freedom from someone else's servant—from someone else's daughter? We are all needed. As Paul said, *"And if they were all one member, where would the body be?"* (1 Cor. 12:19). Paul and Peter made it perfectly clear to us—just in case we're tempted to flex our muscles and get our way—that in Heaven's paradigm, the weaker parts deserve greater honor.

Jockeying for Position

I was once counseled a couple who needed some help managing their young ADHD son. The kid was getting out of hand, and in response, the dad had begun to use a lot of physical discipline. I was trying to teach them how to set healthy limits with natural consequences instead of physical abuse. That's when it came out that the wife was being physically abused as well. The husband would pin her down and spank her with his belt when she wouldn't "obey" him. He was the "head of the house," and as such, he considered it his place to physically discipline his whole household. There are many things I could say about this, but here I'll be brief. This guy had the wrong definition of what it means to be the "head."

The biblical foundation of headship is the Kingdom principle that the weaker, hidden parts—including women and children—deserve greater honor. It is very important that we understand what headship actually means, because if we don't, we will read 1 Corinthians 11:3 as a hierarchy: *"But I want you to know that the head of every man is Christ, the head of woman is man, and the head of Christ is God."* In a hierarchy, *head* becomes a metaphor for "most powerful," the boss. We all like to know who the boss is—the head of the organization or church or family—so we can locate ourselves in the chain of command. And yes, deep down we will admit that we want to be the head.

However, this interpretation is completely at odds with the servant leadership Christ demonstrated when He was on earth. Christ turned everything upside down when He—the boss—set aside His status at the top and led the way to the bottom. And that is the direction we all must go if we want to follow Him: *"If anyone desires to be first, he shall be last of all and servant of all"* (Mark 9:35). Heaven's model is not top-down, but bottom-up: *"You know that those who are considered rulers over the Gentiles lord it over them, and their great ones exercise authority over them. Yet it shall not be so among you; but whoever desires to become great among you shall be your servant"* (Mark 10:42-43).

Jesus' teaching and example alone should be enough to steer us away from patriarchal/hierarchical thinking. Unfortunately, many of us still don't get it. We even go so far as to project a chain of command onto the Trinity. This idea goes all the way back to the fourth century, when a man named Arius of Alexander began teaching that Jesus was subordinate to God.[1] However, orthodox teaching throughout Church.history has affirmed that Jesus is in no way subordinate to the Father. All members of the Trinity are equally God and hold equal authority. So we can hardly imagine the Trinity arguing over who's the boss: "I'm the Father, so what I say goes. You, Son, and You, Holy Spirit, are going to have to duke it out to decide who's going to be number two. I'm number one, and there has to be a one and a two and a three and a four and so forth." That is ludicrous thinking. It just doesn't work like that in Heaven. The Trinity is in perfect unity; the Godhead has no need to jockey for position.

So if *head* doesn't mean the top of a hierarchy, then what does it mean?

In Greek thought, *head* was a metaphor for origin—like the head of a river. They also believed the head was the life source for the body. Thus, in his book *Beyond Sex Roles*, Bible scholar Gilbert Bilezikian suggests that the proper translation of the word for *head* in 1 Corinthians 11:3 is *fountainhead* (or life source). This translation gives rise to two levels of meaning. The first meaning is that each of these pairs—Christ is the head of man, man is the head of woman, God is the head of Christ—is not depicting a hierarchy, but giving a chronological view of creation and salvation history. First came the creation of man, second the formation of woman, and third the birth of Christ.[2] This explains away the troubling suggestions that Christ is subordinate to God, as well as the idea that women are inherently subordinate to men, which the broader message of the Gospel clearly contradicts.[3]

The second level of meaning emerges from the idea that the *head* is the connector and life source for the body. Paul clearly had this idea in mind when he used the metaphor *head* in two passages that describe how Christ, the Head, relates to His Body:

> *But speaking the truth in love, we are to grow up in all aspects into* **Him who is the head**, *even Christ, from whom the whole body, being fitted and held together by what every joint supplies, according to the proper working of each individual part,* **causes the growth of the body for the building up of itself in love.** (Eph. 4:15-16 NASB)

> *Let no one keep defrauding you of your prize by delighting in self-abasement and the worship of the angels, taking his stand on visions he has seen, inflated without cause by his fleshly mind, and not holding fast to* **the head**, *from whom the entire body, being* **supplied** *and* **held together** *by the joints and ligaments, grows with a growth which is from God.* (Col. 2:18-19 NASB)

Clearly, the function of the head is to hold the body together and to facilitate proper growth. It is *not* meant to boss the other parts around.

Biblical headship is not opposed to the idea that the head is a source of power, but it is absolutely opposed to the head withholding that power and using it to dominate or control. Rather, the function of the head is to give its power away—*to empower*. When we are rightly related to Christ, our head, we can do *all things* (see Phil. 4:13). We are completely empowered in our relationship with God. In fact, Jesus said we would do greater works than He did (see John 14:12). He is not in a competition with us to prove His superiority. He is giving us all He has so we can go farther and higher. Similarly, Christ in God is fully empowered as God. Christ is the exact representation of the Father (see Heb. 1:3). It follows that the same principle applies to the relationship between men and women. When Eve was taken from Adam's side, she was formed as a suitable partner (see Gen. 2:18), and given the same authority and the same mission as her husband. She was not diminished or limited by her relationship to Adam. She was fully empowered in their partnership.

The Head of the House

Many women are taught that being good, "submissive" wives means basically having no opinions and allowing their husbands to have the final say in all decisions. They interpret "two becoming one" to mean "two becoming him." This teaching is primarily based on Paul's letter to the Ephesians:

Wives, submit to your own husbands, as to the Lord. For the husband is head of the wife, as also Christ is head of the church; and He is the Savior of the body. Therefore, just as the church is subject to Christ, so let the wives be to their own husbands in everything. Husbands, love your wives, just as Christ also loved the church and gave Himself for her.... (Eph. 5:22-25)

At first glance, this passage seems to teach wives to be subservient to their husbands, while admonishing husbands to love and be compassionate toward their wives as the lesser partner. This hierarchical interpretation seems normal and even obvious, which is why people have such a hard time with it. But a little bit of study to grasp the historical and textual context goes a long way to help us see how this passage fits with Christ's anti-patriarchal paradigm.

Directly following this passage, Paul gives similar instructions about children obeying their parents and slaves obeying their masters (see Eph. 6:1-9). In the Greek and Jewish cultures of Paul's day, it was an accepted fact that men were superior to women, that fathers were superior to children, and that masters were superior to slaves. Children had some value, especially if they were male children, but they were expected to unquestioningly obey their fathers—not just as small children, but as adults as well. Women and slaves were even worse off. They had no rights and served the whim of the ruling male in their environment—father, husband, or master. In a very real and absolute sense, the patriarch ruled. And every man's ambition was to reach the position of ruling male in his family unit in order to have the power.[4]

What Paul wrote to the women, children, and slaves of this culture was completely liberating. It had to have been some of the most shocking language his audience had ever heard. He was messing with the very foundations of his society when he declared that women, children, and slaves had value and that they deserved honor and love. The fact that Paul would tell fathers not to provoke their children was revolutionary (see Eph. 6:4), as was telling masters to show their servants the same respect they expected from them (see Eph. 6:5-9). Paul's command that husbands love their wives and lay down their lives for them was flat-out radical (see Eph. 5:25).

Given the historical context, Paul's command for husbands to love their wives is staggering enough. But it is even more staggering because of what Paul meant by *love*, and this—not wives being submissive—should strike us as the biggest challenge and command in these verses, whether or not we know the historical context. If we could even begin to grasp what this looks like, much less practice it, I'm sure this entire passage would stop troubling everyone. I love how The Message translates this verse:

> *Husbands, go all out in your love for your wives, exactly as Christ did for the church—a love marked by giving, not getting. Christ's love makes the church whole. His words evoke her beauty. Everything he does and says is designed to bring the best out of her, dressing her in dazzling white silk, radiant with holiness. And that is how husbands ought to love their wives.* (Eph. 5:25-28 MSG)

Paul was essentially saying to men, "Okay, you think you're superior? Well, this is what Jesus (who actually *is* superior) did for us, His inferiors. He pursued us with reckless abandon. He gave everything—His very life—to rescue us, restore our dignity and freedom, and clothe us like royalty. He came down to our level so He could raise us up to His level and empower us to reach our full potential in Him. His one ambition as our *head* is to make sure that we are growing, thriving, and successful. That is what it looks like to be a husband in this Kingdom."

Again, if we could get this, the whole submission thing would not be a problem. Wives, how many of you would have a problem receiving the love and following the lead of a man whose one goal in life is to make sure that you are happy, whole, and fulfilling your God-given dreams and potential?

Paul had more to say about what he meant by *love*. Husbands are to love their wives like they love their own bodies: *"So husbands ought to love their own wives as their own bodies; he who loves his wife loves himself. For no one ever hated his own flesh, but nourishes and cherishes it, just as the Lord does the church"* (Eph. 5:28-29). In a culture where women were considered property, telling a man to love his wife like his body was a significant shift. On the other side of women's liberation, we read these verses and think, *Dang, honey, you were born female; that's rough.* However, Paul was saying just the opposite. He was promoting women to equal status in marriage and honoring them as intrinsically valuable beings. He did the same in 1 Corinthians 7:4, which says, *"The wife does not have authority over her own body, but the husband does. And likewise the husband does not have authority over his own body, but the wife does."*

This idea of a wife having authority over her husband's body, which again was absolutely counter-cultural in the first century, flows directly from Paul's understanding that Christian marriage is an equal partnership. He is exactly in line with Christ's teaching that marriage is an indissoluble, mutual relationship between two equally valuable people:

> *"Have you not read that He who made them at the beginning made them male and female, and said, 'For this reason a man shall leave his father and mother and be joined to his wife, and the two shall become one flesh'? So then they are no longer two but one flesh. Therefore what God has joined together, let not man separate."* (Matt. 19:4-6)

In God's version of marriage, the husband belongs to the wife just as much as the wife belongs to the husband, *because they are one flesh.* The husband loves himself by loving his wife, and the wife loves herself by loving her husband, *because they are one flesh.*

The mystery of marriage, Paul says, reflects the mystery of the "one flesh" union Christ has created between Himself and us: *"For no one ever hated his own flesh, but nourishes and cherishes it, just as the Lord does the church. For we are members of His body and His flesh and of His bones"* (Eph. 5:29-30). Paul is using covenant language to describe a covenant reality. Christ, our Bridegroom, loves us as He loves Himself. He has elevated us to the status of an equal, eternal covenant partner with Him. We are the Bride of Christ. There is no higher position for humanity, and no greater love in the universe than the love of our Bridegroom—our Head—for us. And our marriages should follow this pattern.

Every man has to fight for love to win in his heart so that he can function as a true Christ-like head to his wife and his family. When I met my oldest child, my daughter Brittney, just after she was born, I was overwhelmed by her smallness. I felt this ache in my core that, if I could put words to it, felt something like this: "I am so scared of you! I feel so vulnerable, so underequipped. But I can't remember ever feeling love like this before, either. I will do anything for you!" Even though I felt terrified by my feelings of powerlessness and the many ways in which this little child could potentially hurt me in the future, I was compelled by my love for her. Now that Brittney is a grown woman, my love for her continues to compel me to do all that I can to empower her in my environment. That is what love does to us—if we will let it.

Okay, so now that we understand what Paul meant when he told husbands to love their wives, what are we supposed to do with the command for the wife to submit to her husband? First of all, let me clarify that the husband is in no way supposed to compete with God. That would be idolatrous.[5] Instead, the wife is meant to submit to her husband in a way similar to how she submits to God.[6] In the New Covenant, our devotion to the Lord comes from love, not from fear. Christ came to earth as a servant, and He loved us to life. Our response to His servant love is mutual servant love—not only toward Him, but in all our relationships with one another, just as He commanded: *This is my commandment, that you love one another as I have loved you* (John 15:12). This is why Paul first commanded mutual submission between all the believers (see Eph. 5:21), and then specifically highlighted the relationships between wives and husbands, children and parents, and masters and servants. All these relationships are to express mutual love and submission—willing servanthood. Thus, when the wife submits, she does so as a response to love—not in response to fear.

Submission out of fear—demanded rather than willingly offered servanthood—will never bring about intimacy or heart connection. I knew a couple who had some pretty serious marital issues because whenever the husband wanted sex, he would say, "It is time for you to service your husband." The wife felt so humiliated and degraded by his inference that it was her obligation to perform a sexual service because she was his wife. Unsurprisingly, their marriage had no intimacy or affection, only pain and disconnection. If her husband had approached her with love instead of demands, he would have created the opportunity for his wife to freely respond to his love, and their marriage (and sex life) would have been a lot happier and healthier.

The truth is that submission out of fear—required submission—is an oxymoron. *Submission* has morphed into *subjugation*. We have lost the essence of biblical submission because scared people have demanded it instead of offering it. But we need our word back, because it's a very important word. It is a big part of the Christian life—for all of us. We are all called to submit *to each other* and *to Christ*. But that doesn't mean obeying so we don't get punished or the big yellow dump truck flattening the little red pickup.[7] The Greek word for "submission," *hypotasso*, "was a Greek military term meaning 'to arrange [troop divisions] in a military fashion under the command of a leader.' In non-military use, it was 'a voluntary attitude of giving in, cooperating, assuming responsibility, and carrying a burden.'"[8] When Paul said, *"Submit to one another out of reverence for Christ"* (Eph. 5:21), he was saying, "We are all following the same leader, and He wants us to arrange our lives so that we voluntarily keep in step with one another. No more wandering off and doing your own thing. We are in this *together*, and we need to make sure no man, woman, or child is left behind."

True *submission* is a powerful relational dynamic where we live in a way that prioritizes connection. When we submit, we work hard to protect our relationship and avoid actions that hurt it. We stay open to one another's influence by paying attention to one another's thoughts, needs, and feelings so we can preserve a continual harmony of hearts.

This understanding of submission works beautifully with the understanding that true headship is about taking care of the body and making sure that each part is receiving proper attention and honor so that they work together well (see 1 Cor 12:19-27). If a part of the physical body is broken or suffering, the head doesn't just move on. It can't. It is connected to the body, and it suffers when the body suffers. It follows that a man's role as a head of his family is to steward the honor and health of the family members, guaranteeing that his wife and children live powerful and free lives around him and in society.

Finding a Helper

We now need to examine one last word: *helper*. We have defined *helper* as "servant" or "assistant" by seeing it through a patriarchal lens. However, this was not at all what God meant when He said, *"It is not good for the man to be alone; I will make him a helper suitable for him"* (Gen. 2:18 NASB). Here the word translated "suitable" literally means "comparable to,"[9] equal and complementary.

None of the animals could take away Adam's loneliness, because they did not fit with him—they were not his equal. God made Adam in His likeness, designed to be in intimate relationship with someone who was part of him and inseparable from him—mirroring the perfect union of the Trinity. Eve was created from Adam's side as the missing piece in this picture, the *only* perfect match for Adam. Together, she and Adam represented the image of God: *"God created human beings; he created them godlike, reflecting God's nature. He created them male and female"* (Gen. 1:27 MSG).

When we see Adam and Eve as the joint reflection of God, we understand that *helper* cannot mean, "Hey Adam, here's your housekeeper and bed-warmer. Here's someone to kick around when you've had a bad day." I believe God meant something more like, "Hey Adam, here's your other half who fits perfectly with you. She's going to make it possible for you to experience the relationship and intimacy I designed you for. And the bonus is, she's super helpful, which is a good thing, because you're going to need it!"

Jesus said something very similar when He promised a Helper for His disciples—the Holy Spirit. He didn't tell them the Holy Spirit would be their supernatural bellboy or someone they could boss around. Rather, Jesus promised His disciples, "I'm going to leave you One who comes alongside, who reminds, and who convicts. I'm going to send you an intercessor, a consoler, an advocate, a comforter, a teacher, a counselor. I'm going to leave you a Helper" (see John 14:16, 26; 15:26). Not only that, Jesus called this Helper the "Spirit of truth" and implied that it's better to have the Helper around than to have Jesus in the flesh (see John 15:26; 16:17). That means the Helper is pretty important.

The Hebrew noun translated as "help" or "helper," *ezer*, is used twenty-one times in the Old Testament, and of these, two are used to describe Eve, three are used to describe military help, and the rest are used to describe God.[10] The verb form, *azar*, is used another eighty times, often as a description of God.[11] God was setting Eve in pretty good company when He referred to her as Adam's helper, because He Himself is called humanity's Helper.

The Ministry of Reconciliation

We must come to grips with the reality that *helper* does not in any way imply *inferior*. A helper is someone who offers something vital and irreplaceable—something we cannot offer ourselves and desperately need. Boiled down,

I'll say here that I believe the role of the helper relates to reconciliation. We see this in the Holy Spirit's work in us when we get saved. As the great Helper, He reconciles us to God, and then He gives us the ministry of reconciliation to others:

> *Therefore, if anyone is in Christ, he is a new creation; old things have passed away; behold, all things have become new. Now all things are of God, who has reconciled us to Himself through Jesus Christ, and has given us the ministry of reconciliation.* (2 Cor. 5:17-18)

Within the Body of Christ, helpers are called to unify us in our differences. Throughout Church history, we haven't done a very good job at unity, and I believe one big reason for this is that we have suppressed the women. Women, our helpers, are particularly gifted as reconcilers and builders of relationship.

The recent history of Rwanda illustrates this point. After the 1994 genocide, in which 800,000 people were brutally killed in just 100 days, Rwanda was left with a significant female majority in the population. The genocide had primarily been planned and executed by men, and a large number of those killed or later jailed for their crimes were men. When the country began picking up the pieces, the women rose to the forefront as the leaders in reconciliation and peace. Though Rwanda remains a very patriarchal society, the facts of their history forced a shift and gave women a unique opportunity to demonstrate the strengths of femininity. Now, women fill 42 percent of the government seats in Rwanda. (The U.S. government is only 16 percent female.) And they have been, in large part, responsible for the degree of healing that has happened in Rwanda in the last two decades.[12]

The reconciling and peace-making role of the helper is very important to our health as a society. It's time for us men to stop using "headship" as a trump card and start imitating Jesus, our true Head, in becoming life-giving servant leaders who get behind and under our women in order to facilitate them as they play this vital role.

Chapter Six

THE GIFTS OF WOMEN

*S*everal years ago, Kris Vallotton and I visited a church in South America to talk to the men about women in leadership. On a previous trip to this church, Kris had initiated a discussion on this topic, and let's just say that talk had *not* gone well. This country is firmly patriarchal. The ceiling above the women's heads is not made of glass, but of brass. Women have little power or influence in either the Church or the nation, and they certainly *were not* incorporated in the leadership of this church. Therefore, it wasn't terribly surprising that the leaders of the church reacted strongly against Kris's ideas about women. "You are contradicting what the Bible teaches!" they protested.

On this second trip, Kris and I had a goal to reveal the importance of empowering women. In the end, he explained it in a way that I thought was a word of wisdom from Heaven. "In a single-parent family," he pointed out, "one element is missing—either the father or the mother. If the mother is absent, the father is forced to try to be both mother *and* father to his children, but when he tries to step into the role of mother, he compromises his ability to be who he's called to be as a father. In order for a family to be whole, a mother and a father must both be present and fulfilling their roles."

"The Church has been like a motherless family," Kris continued. "The father—the male leadership—has been trying really hard to be both mother and father, but he's not created to do that. Thus, the male leaders in the Church have never really been able to be the father—the man—in the Church because they've also been trying to be the mother."

The room was silent. Seeing that he had clearly captured the attention of these pastors, Kris nailed his final point: "Empowering women releases men to step into their destiny and identity. When men are no longer trying, unsuccessfully, to fulfill both roles, they will be freed to be who God created them to be. Together—with the men acting as men and the women acting as women—they can work to create a family."

Kris struck home. The leaders of the church were weeping in repentance and joy at this vision of the Church family functioning in wholeness and unity.

That vision and goal is my passion. I want nothing more than to empower women and, by doing so, to empower men, too. Why? Because when that happens, the Church will look the way Jesus wants her to look—a whole, healthy, beautiful bride with all the members living the fulfilling, powerful lives they were created to fulfill.

Partnerships at the Bottom, Not One Guy at the Top

As I discussed in *Culture of Honor*, I believe an apostolic reformation is taking place in the Body of Christ. For a long time, we've run around with a pastor and teacher-driven government. That means we usually have a hierarchy with one or maybe a few powerful people at the top and everyone else working to keep the powerful people happy.[1] This is not God's design. His design is the apostles and prophets as the foundation, with Jesus as the cornerstone (see Eph. 2:20)—an image that is very similar to the Greek image of the *head* as the supporter and sustainer. Apostolic government, as Christ modeled and instructed, is positioned at the bottom of the pyramid. It supports, equips, and empowers. One man is never sufficient for the role. Only a team with diverse gifts will do—that is why Paul gives us his lists of apostles, prophets, teachers, pastors, and so forth. in Ephesians 4 and 1 Corinthians 12. Apostolic leaders have a God-given ability to unify team members with a wide diversity of gifts and roles to serve a common mission. And that mission is to realize Heaven's blueprint for establishing the Kingdom on earth. In an apostolic culture, more and more people experience the freedom to "happen" because they are being equipped and empowered by apostolic leadership and *sent* ("apostle" means "sent one") into their sphere of influence with power and Kingdom strategies.

The image of a team with unique yet equally vital roles works in perfect harmony with the image of every believer being a unique and equally vital member of the Body of Christ. But I think we can add another dimension to the picture of apostolic government by understanding that the Church, while being a Body, is also a family. The same principles and characteristics apply to God's original design for the human family in the Garden. Adam and Eve were given equal authority and responsibility as the mother and father of humanity. The patriarch was never to be without a matriarch at his side, co-leading the family. They were partners. Each brought unique but equally valuable perspectives and gifts to the table in nurturing and raising their children.

This picture of "team" leadership is a reflection of the Trinity. A family—a council of equal Persons who live to bring each other glory—governs our universe, not a top-down, loner God. The love and partnership in the Trinity is a great mystery, but we can see enough of it to know that if we are truly seeking to imitate it in the Body of Christ, we will not have one man at the top. We will have a team—a team made up of people who are God-appointed and have God-given ministry callings and gifts. That team will also have a balanced gender ratio, effectively bringing both mothering and fathering into the Body.

Putting Up the Screen

In order to move toward this kind of apostolic, family-oriented leadership model, we need a renewed vision of gender from Heaven, a vision that on one hand is gender-blind, and yet on the other hand accurately perceives and appreciates gender distinctions.

Malcolm Gladwell uses a beautiful illustration of the value of gender-blindness—the kind of gender-blindness I think we need in the Church when it comes to recognizing those God has called to be leaders. In *Blink*, he draws his readers' attention to the world of classical music, a world that, "over the past few decades...has undergone a revolution."[2] This revolution began in the 60s' and 70s', when orchestra musicians began to demand that the hiring process be more regulated and egalitarian. As a result, many orchestras began to hold blind auditions, where the players auditioned from behind a screen to remove any visual distractions. When these blind auditions became standard, "an extraordinary thing happened: orchestras began to hire women. In the past thirty years...the number of women in the top U.S. orchestras has increased fivefold."[3] Screens exposed the powerbrokers of the classical music world to a reality they had been unconscious of for centuries, the reality that *what they were hearing was absolutely and hopelessly infected by what they were seeing*. When they couldn't see the women auditioning, they finally heard them.[4]

Gender-blindness can be fairly simple to achieve in specific, crucial moments—as simple as putting up a screen—but difficult to sustain over longer periods. This is demonstrated by the case of trombone player Abbie Conant. While Conant was given a job with the Munich Philharmonic after playing behind a screen, she ended up facing a lengthy battle to keep it. She was demoted, forced to perform various medical tests to demonstrate her fitness (which was exemplary), made to play for a trombone expert (who gave her rave reviews), and then, after regaining first chair, had to lobby for equal pay with her colleagues.[5]

In the face of what has always been, it's hard to hold onto those unbiased moments when we perceive what could be—especially when what could be doesn't immediately seem attractive. If it threatens our position, makes us look bad, or offends some deep-seated sensibility of what's "natural" (e.g., women are just not built to play large brass instruments...or to pastor churches), then we will resist the truth of those moments. But truth is truth, and at some point we need to realize that we are going to look pretty dumb if we keep clinging to an old, flawed value system after seeing it for what it is.

There are two big attractions that should draw us toward pursuing gender-blindness in developing, hiring, and promoting church leaders. Number one: *It's the right thing to do*. The qualifications for church leaders are not defined by gender. A church leader is qualified by character, gifts, and calling. Last time I checked, God is still gifting and calling both men *and* women to preach, teach, administrate, counsel, pray, walk in purity of character, build teams, and do any other job required of any church leadership position—even senior positions. Heidi Baker is a perfect example of a woman God has called to be an apostolic leader. God sent her to Africa, but that doesn't mean He isn't raising up other female apostles to lead here in the States.

If we accept that pursuing gender-blindness is the right thing to do, then attraction number two is obvious: *Being gender-blind in choosing our church leaders increases our chances of appointing those who are most qualified.* I wonder if at any point, after they started hiring more and more women, all those conductors and music directors asked themselves, "How long have we been missing out on having some of the best musicians play in our orchestra simply because, due to our gender bias, we couldn't really hear them?" I know I've been asking that question myself when it comes to church leadership. Gender bias is, I believe, responsible not only for disqualifying many gifted women from leadership; it has also qualified many men who are not really gifted as leaders.

Where Gender Matters

The family of God needs fathers and mothers. This is where we need to gain fresh appreciation for gender distinctions. Mothering and fathering are gendered roles, so we need to understand how gender comes into play. When we look at God's design for the family, we see that men and women make equally important, though different, contributions in order to become parents. Both are equally responsible to nurture and raise their children. Parenting is a complementary partnership where mom and dad each contribute equally important, though different, pieces.

There has been a trend in the last few decades towards greater gender-blindness in parenting. Many people now recognize that most jobs in a family can be fulfilled by either gender. However, it does not follow that children don't actually need both of their parents, which is what many people in our culture are trying to prove. The results of divorce and single parenting don't lie. The gold standard for giving children the best chance at success in life is still the nuclear family, in which children are raised by their biological mother and father.

While fathers and mothers can certainly perform equally well in most jobs, both in the home and the workplace, gender makes a distinct impact in the different ways mothers and fathers socialize and relate to their children. These differences emerge instinctively from the moment babies come into the world. Mothers cuddle their babies; dads throw them in the air. Mothers are constantly communicating verbally and visually with their children, while dads engage them in the realm of action. Mothers care about safety and stability; fathers want their children to take risks and test their limits. These are obviously generalizations, but they are commonly recognizable and support the point that mothers and fathers contribute different aspects to their children's development that balance one another and help to create well-rounded human beings. Similarly, I believe that mothers and fathers in the Church, while being equally capable of fulfilling the job demands of a leadership role, bring unique social and relational elements to their styles of leadership that the Body desperately needs in order to grow mature and healthy.

In order to partner successfully together, mothers and fathers, both in the natural family and in the Church, need to be sufficiently mature and skilled in appreciating, making room for, and cooperating with one another's differences. Perhaps the greatest significance of gender in parenting is that it is the central aspect of how mothers and fathers raise their children to be able to honor, appreciate, and work with other people who are different than they are. And parents will only teach this to the degree that they themselves have learned to do it. If they are not capable of sustaining a healthy partnership with one another, they will pass broken patterns of relating on to their children. Unfortunately, this seems to be the norm. But the Church is called to break those patterns and replace them with healthy ones. This is why it is so crucial for our leadership to model healthy partnerships, *especially* between men and women.

In general, working with other people is challenging—even when we run with people who are very similar to us. But these challenges climb to a whole new level when men and women try to work together. There is no doubt, both scientifically and in experience, that men and women are wired differently. We think about life differently, see situations and people differently, and need different things in order to feel successful and fulfilled in life. This isn't just true in marriage, but in male-female relationships in general.

For the most part, we men like working primarily with other men because it seems easier. We have the same sense of humor, the same priorities, the same reasoning processes, and the same ways of dealing with stress and disagreements. For the most part, men have the same needs for significance and respect, and we communicate our needs and desires in similar ways. Not all men are the same, but we're a lot more like each other than we are like most women, and those similarities make it comfortable and safe for us to work together. For many of us, the idea of incorporating women in our Church leadership—as peers with equal or even greater authority—feels scary. We think, *Oh no! Those women do crazy things that don't make any sense. There's no way I am giving them power in my environment!* The ways women are different cause us to view them as unpredictable and, therefore, unstable and unsafe. Thus we surround ourselves only with powerful men and create very high fences to keep women out.

However, this fear is actually a sign that we are not mature or powerful. If femininity intimidates us, then we men need to grow up—and address the brokenness in our hearts. Unfortunately, due to patriarchal parenting, most men are raised to see masculinity and femininity not as opposites that attract, but as opposites that conflict. We learn simplistic pairs of apparently opposing characteristics—women are emotional and men are analytical, for example—and then, because we want to feel confident in our male identity, we think, "Emotions are feminine and I don't want to be a woman, so I'm not going to be emotional and I'm definitely not going to listen to or try to understand a woman when she's being emotional." Obviously, this kind of black-and-white thinking categorically defeats partnership between the genders, which is *not* God's design for us. He wants us to grow up and learn to see how our opposites were designed not to limit partnership, but to attract and facilitate it.

God designed our differences to work together, which means we need to learn to value them and invite them to be fully expressed in our relationships. Men, instead of putting everything "female" in the "I can have nothing to do with this because I'm a man" category, we need to put it in the "you have something I don't have, which I need" category. We need to appreciate and understand the nuances of a woman's sensitivity to emotions and how this trait is specifically designed to meet a deep need in us. And the same is true for women. Women need to appreciate and understand the nuances of a men's ability to analyze and compartmentalize their feelings and thoughts and how this trait is specifically designed to meet a deep need in them. God wants us to do this with every one of our complementary differences. Doing so trains us to become mature men and women who are vulnerable enough to say, "I can't do what you can do. I need what you bring to the table. I need your opinions and your perspective. Please share them with me, and I will do my best to listen and respond with honor."

God told us that He created both men and women to bear His image, meaning that if we only allow the men to have influence or value, we are only valuing half of who God is and what He placed in humanity. We are like a person with two working eyes who puts a patch over one eye and walks through life with one-eyed vision.[6] If we want to step into the fullness of what God has for us, we need to take off the patch and begin walking with both eyes open. We need to empower women to be who they are and to bring the unique aspects of God that are imbedded in femininity.

Strengths of Femininity

Thanks to the male insecurity driving the patriarchal paradigm, the world and the Church have long maintained a negative stereotype of femininity. We see this in "blonde jokes" (which are really "female jokes") and in common descriptors like silly, frivolous, airhead, Barbie, uninformed, too talkative, complicated, overly emotional, flighty, illogical, and so forth. Women, like men, have areas of weakness. However, our culture has far too often amplified the areas of weakness or difference in women to the point that being a woman is accompanied by a chorus of negative adjectives. By valuing male characteristics more than female ones, we have created an environment where it is very difficult for a woman to be successful and influential without suppressing her femininity. Hillary Clinton is an excellent example of this. Remember when she was on the campaign trail, and she happened to shed a few tears talking about how stressful campaigning was? The media ate her up like a swarm of sharks, all because she was vulnerable and cried. Her tears did not make her any less valuable or capable. They were simply the natural reaction women have when they are stressed. When women have to become like men in order to be trusted and empowered, it is a lose-lose scenario. The men miss out on the dimensions of God conveyed by femininity, and the women aren't fulfilled because they're trying to be something they're not.

The world is finally beginning to recognize that female strengths—things like intuition and compassion for others—are significant strengths in leadership,[7] but we still have a lot of work to do in recognizing the value of femininity. When I interviewed the powerful women I told you about in Chapter 3, I asked them what they thought were particularly women's strengths in a leadership setting. Here are some of the strengths they listed:

- Women are more intuitive and have a different sensitivity to the Holy Spirit.

- Women are generally more emotionally intelligent and aware of their own well-being and the well-being of those around them.[8]

- Women have a "transformational" type of leadership. They are concerned about personal development in their staff, not just about performance.[9]

- Women are concerned about and aware of how their decisions will affect others.

- Women are good at giving specific affirmation and are nurturing, sympathetic, and inclusive. No one is left behind.

- Women tend to be good listeners. They are relational, patient, and compassionate, and they value teamwork. They bring the positives of the family lifestyle into the work environment.[10]

- Women are great at multitasking, which enables them to simultaneously perform tasks, hold conversation, and mentally problem-solve.[11]

- Women tend to think globally—they look for how decisions will play out systemically and generationally.

- Women are also good at administration and details, seeing the necessary steps along the way to accomplish the goal.

- Women want win-win, while men tend to just want to win. This means that many women are great moderators.

- Women have less ego and are not as concerned with receiving recognition. They are often quicker to self-sacrifice for the good of the organization or the vision.

- Women are often fearless (the mama bear instinct), as well as resolute and unwilling to veer from the truth.

- Women possess creativity, thrift, and ingenuity, which makes them great at coming up with effective solutions.

These, obviously, are generalities. Some men are better at each of these things than some women. However, it is true that many women tend to excel in these areas. Women bring something powerful to the table, and we are missing out when we exclude them.

Women are receiving more and more acclaim regarding their leadership and managerial abilities. A recent study by Zenger and Folkman, an authority on strengths-based leadership development, found that women excelled more than men in a majority of leadership areas. These included areas, like "driving for results," that are typically considered male turf.[12] In his book *Man Down*, lawyer Dan Abrams collected data from multiple studies to highlight the unexpected ways women counter stereotypes and surpass men in performance. His subtitle says it all: *Proof Beyond a Reasonable Doubt That Women Are Better Cops, Drivers, Gamblers, Spies, World Leaders, Beer Tasters, Hedge Fund Managers, and Just About Everything Else.* According to Abrams, the studies show that genetically, women are made to be excellent at a lot of things men aren't so excellent at.[13]

I am not suggesting that women are fundamentally better than men, as many feminists do. I am simply stating that men and women have equal worth and that our differences complement each other. We belong together. And we *do* work well together when we stop listening to our gender fears and learn to appreciate our coordinating strengths.

Feminine Intuition

One powerful trait in most women is their unique sensitivity to the movement of the Holy Spirit. When the wind of the Spirit begins to blow in an environment, usually women sense it first. I can often tell when the Spirit is moving because I see the women starting to come undone. When I see them responding to His Presence in a meeting, I know it's time to get ready for the Holy Spirit to do something. I'm not saying that men don't sense the Holy Spirit—obviously, they do. However, I believe women have a unique sensitivity that is often quicker and more perceptive. Tragically, in many parts of the Church throughout history and even today, this sensitivity to the Spirit has been labeled "emotionalism" and has been squelched.

Another aspect of feminine spiritual sensitivity manifests in an uncanny ability to know what's really going on in an environment and what should or should not be done. We see a classic example of "how to make a really bad decision because you didn't heed female intuition" when Jesus was on trial before Pilate. Pilate's wife sent him a message: *"Have nothing to do with that just Man, for I have suffered many things today in a dream because of Him"* (Matt. 27:19). But instead of listening to his wife, Pilate gave in to fear of the people and gave the order for Jesus to be crucified.

Later on in that chapter, we see that women had a greater perception regarding who Jesus was, and they acted on their perception while the men reacted to the situation in fear. Matthew 27:55 says,

And many women who followed Jesus from Galilee, ministering to Him, were there looking on from afar, among whom were Mary Magdalene, Mary the mother of James and Joses, and the mother of Zebedee's sons.

The men took off running, but the women kept following Jesus and stayed with Him even as He was crucified. After Jesus had died and was buried, the women continued following Him. As Joseph of Arimathea buried Jesus's body, Mary Magdalene and the other Mary were sitting opposite the tomb, waiting (see Matt. 27:61). Somehow, it seems, they knew this wasn't the end of the story. Three days later, they came back to discover that an earthquake had split the rocks and an angel had rolled away the stone from the entrance of the tomb (see Matt. 28:1-3). The angel told the women to go and find the disciples—who were hiding somewhere—and tell them that Jesus had risen (see Matt. 28:5-10).

I wonder whether the women, rather than the men, were the ones to discover the empty tomb because of their spiritual intuition. Why else would they be drawn to visit and linger in such a dangerous place while the disciples were hiding in fear in their homes?

Most husbands can tell stories of times they ignored their wives' intuition, to their later regret. I certainly can. Once, when our daughter, Brittney, was five years old, she fell off the countertop of an outdoor kitchen and landed on her face on the concrete patio. She split her chin, so I took her inside and put butterfly bandages on the cut. I also checked her teeth and mouth to see if I could detect any areas of concern. Everything looked fine to me. But Sheri wasn't so sure. She really wanted to take Britt to the hospital to get an X-ray. We had been planning to leave that day for an overnight trip to an amusement park. Seeing that the hospital would put a definite wrinkle in our itinerary, I said, "Let's wait and see how she does." We waited about an hour, and Britt seemed to be fine. We decided to leave for our trip.

Later that night, at the hotel, Britt woke up crying. Sheri's intuition kicked in, and she said, "Something is wrong!"

"She's just trying to get attention," I said. I figured her jaw was sore from her fall and she was trying to use her injury to her advantage. I prevailed, and we put Britt back to sleep and continued on as normal.

The next day, while we were at the amusement park, I bought Britt a piece of candy. Later I noticed that she was still carrying it around. "Britt," I said, "why aren't you eating your candy?"

"My mouth hurts," she said. She refused to eat it. At that point, I realized that something was wrong—what kid won't eat candy? Still, I was sure it couldn't be *that* serious. After a full day at the park, we drove home late Sunday night. The next morning, we finally took Britt to the doctor. When the doctor examined her, he said, "It doesn't look like anything's broken, but let's do an X-ray anyway." He and I were shocked by the results—and Sheri started crying because she had been right all along. Her baby girl had been walking around for two days with a *broken jaw!*

Britt spent the next three weeks with her mouth wired shut, and I learned a valuable lesson about heeding my wife's intuition.

If we're honest, most of us men are at least a little bit scared of female intuition and sensitivity. It feels too undefined and out of our control. It seems like a great way for our women to have the reins and get their own way. It feels like a threat to our power. I certainly have felt scared of feminine intuition before. But when I recognized that fear, I confessed it and repented for it. I decided to change my heart. Now I see the strength of feminine intuition, and I want input from women in my life to help me stay pointed toward the Holy Spirit.

This is not only important in our personal lives and relationships, but in the corporate life of the Church. As the Body of Christ, one of our top priorities is being led by the Spirit. This is a non-negotiable necessity if we want to bring Heaven's agenda and government to earth. We value prophets and prophecy because they help us hear what God is saying. It only makes sense that we should also value female intuition. It's a unique gift of God, given to the ladies, to help us all walk in step with the Spirit so that we get where we want to go and avoid pitfalls and setbacks. Unfortunately, for the most part, we have not valued intuition in the Church. This needs to change. We need to see the incredible value in it and choose, on purpose, to protect this uniquely feminine gift. We need to give feminine intuition a seat at the table where the big decisions are being made.

Champions of Connection

In the last chapter, I highlighted the history of Rwanda and the powerful role women played in bringing peace and reconciliation to their war-torn country. This affinity for reconciliation in women is commonly acknowledged. But it has not been until recently that social scientists studied the source of this feminine strength. When studying the effects of stress on men and women, UCLA researchers found that men under stress exhibit a "fight-or-flight" response that is generally anti-social. They either aggressively get in someone's face or hole up on their own. Women experience the same fight-or-flight feelings in response to stress, but they tend to respond in pro-social ways—hanging out with their kids or talking with a friend. Women combat stress through relational connecting.

These different responses in men and women are shaped by our hormones. When stressed, all of us release a hormone called oxytocin, which increases bonding and decreases anxiety. However, the female hormone, estrogen, amplifies the effects of oxytocin, while testosterone, the male hormone, suppresses them. This accounts for why women under stress reach out for connection, which helps them to calm down and facilitates relational bonding in the process, while men do just the opposite. This also explains why women are good at reconciliation and peace-making, which are most needed in high-stress situations.[14]

A male-dominated world is an imbalanced world. We who have a revelation of God's divine plan for unity between men and women should understand this better than anyone. Dee Dee Myers, writes:

> The simple fact is: Men and women often experience the world differently…When we include and respect these different points of view…we broaden the dialogue, expand the scope of inquiry, change the way we think. We make business more efficient. We make government more responsive. We get better art, better science, better schools. In short, everybody wins. But it starts with accepting the differences.[15]

We are at our best when we find a way to work together. Any organization or church needs *both* men and women working together as powerful peers.

Only then will we have access to *all* of the strengths within humanity and the necessary checks and balances for the weaknesses we all carry. Only then will we all win.

Chapter Seven

POWERFUL PARTNERSHIPS

In Proverbs 31, King Lemuel recounts the advice of a wise and influential woman: his mother. She raised him to be the leader he was, and he made her words famous—words that have inspired countless discussions and debates on what it means to be a "Proverbs 31 woman." The "good woman" this king's mother described looks nothing like a powerless dishwasher. She is a force of nature, presiding over the little kingdom of her home, family, and community with tireless industry, business acumen, relational and emotional intelligence, grace, generosity, and dignity. She is a dreamer and creator, full of plans and strategies that she pursues with initiative and confidence. She is definitely a free and powerful person who is *happening*.

Some people have complained that the Proverbs 31 woman is just another example of the fictional, impossible "ideal woman" that ambitious women are always trying hopelessly to emulate. But this interpretation overlooks a very important element in this picture, namely that the Proverbs 31 woman is happening in a partnership. She has a Proverbs 31 man at her side, who *"trusts her without reserve, and never has reason to regret it"* (Prov. 31:11 MSG). This man is not some hen-pecked weakling, either; he is a leader in his city, and *"is greatly respected when he deliberates with the city fathers"* (Prov. 31:23 MSG). Proverbs 31 is a picture of what a powerful woman can do when she joins forces with a powerful man who believes in her and who, rather than being intimidated by her strengths, praises her for them, knowing that they are one of the reasons he is so respected. She makes him look like a genius, and he does the same for her.

If there's anyone who could tell the Body of Christ what we have to gain by empowering women, as well as how to build successful partnerships with them, it would probably be this Proverbs 31 man. And thankfully, it just so happens that I know some men like him—powerful men who are either married to and/or partnering with powerful women who are currently leading in churches, international ministries, and the marketplace. Several of these guys, as well as a couple of their wives, graciously agreed to open up and let you in on what it's like inside these powerful relationships—specifically, what it looks like to empower, "cover," and protect a powerful woman, how they have dealt with challenges and insecurity, and the benefits of running with an equal, complementary partner.

Making Her Dreams Come True

Skyler Smith is on the senior leadership team of Jesus Culture and is a member of the Jesus Culture band. Skyler is married to Kim Walker-Smith, one of Jesus Culture's lead singers and an internationally renowned worship leader and songwriter. In addition to her extensive schedule leading worship, Kim is active in leadership in the Jesus Culture ministry and music label, fostering new artists and planning recording projects.

"My wife is a natural leader," says Skyler. "She's definitely in the spotlight, but just because you're in the spotlight doesn't mean you have the tools to lead or are valued as a leader. My wife is a leader not just because of the position she has but because of who she is. People are always following her—even people who don't have connection with her. They keep track of what she does and how she responds to things. We're always getting people's comments on how she's living life, which shows that people aren't just following her because she has a title, but because they want to be led by her. She carries what she has on her so well."

From the beginning of their relationship, Skyler could see that Kim walked in a significant measure of authority, authority entrusted to her not solely on the basis of her gifts and skills, but on the basis of her character and favor with God. When I asked Skyler what made Kim a powerful person, he said he saw her power expressed most clearly in the way she carries this authority: "Kim's not afraid to leverage her strength—not in an arrogant or controlling manner, but with confidence and purpose. 'I have things I've got to do, and I'm going to use the tools at hand to get them done.' She's not afraid to dream of things to do and then go after them—regardless of the cost or the commitment. To me, the mark of a powerful person is that you can overcome your fears and actually make your dreams happen."

What does it look like to empower an already powerful person who is going after her God-given purpose and dreams? "I empower my wife by pushing her to be the best she can be all the time," says Skyler. "I will always be the one challenging her to be better and expecting more out of her. When it's hard for her, I encourage her to press through and continue growing in every area. I know I'm doing a great job of empowering Kim when she feels powerful to pursue the things in her heart. I'm not going to make her feel powerful if I'm putting an expectation on her that is not what she is feeling in her heart. But when I'm getting behind the things she feels are right and giving my input, advice, and direction, she feels my strength behind her completely. Then I have a happy wife who knows she can take on the world because she has my support to lean on. The stress, fear, and self-protection go away because she knows I'm there to back her up and take on anybody who's taking her on."

Sustaining this empowering role, Skyler acknowledged, requires a lot of self-confidence, as well as trust that as he's faithful to get behind Kim and her dreams, his own needs and desires will be met. "I need to hold to the belief that regardless of how much influence, popularity, or spotlight Kim has, it's only going to affect me in a good way if that's what the Lord has put on her," he said. "As soon as I start to get derailed or discontent in where I am personally, possibly because of where she is, I've already started to lose the battle, and she will in turn reap the deficit. It's part of my mandate as an equipping and powerful husband to keep myself in that place of being a confident supporter."

From the beginning of their relationship, Kim and Skyler agreed that marriage was a commitment "never to look at life as some competition, but to understand that we were one unit trying to accomplish one goal." Soon after they started dating, Skyler explained his perspective on this to Kim. "I am totally for you achieving your goals, and I'm going to do whatever it takes for you to achieve those goals," he told her. "If that looks like serving you and your vision for this amount of time, or you serving me and my vision for this amount of time, or it looks like you're in the spotlight or I'm in the spotlight or we're in the spotlight together, it all doesn't really matter, because we're both for the best in each other."

So far in their marriage, Kim has been the one more visible and "in front" as a leader. But Skyler says he's comfortable in the supporting role. "I don't need to be in charge or out in front all the time. I need to recognize what the Lord is doing, and then trust Him fully. If He has her out in front at this time, then that's the best thing for her and me. Kim's face being out there right now doesn't have any bearing on my value. I define my identity by who God says I am and what He's asked me to accomplish. If I don't believe we're heading in that direction, I leverage my influence to change it so that we are doing the right thing. But as long as I'm feeling that we're in the right spot, then I'm going to put all my effort into making it go off as good as it can be. Maybe one of the greatest things I ever do in my life is to push my wife as far as I can push her and support her as far as I can support her. I'm okay with that. I'm great with that. That's a great accomplishment."

Leading Together

New Zealand natives Andy and Janine Mason are co-authors of the book Dream Culture and lead the Dream Coaching Program at Bethel Church, which now offers coaching resources, workshops, and training to many organizations around the world.

"My wife and I are equally influential and take turns going in front," Andy explains, though he recognizes that "Janine is also a strong advisory leader—leading alongside as compared to leading from the front alone." He can list many traits that make Janine powerful as a person and a leader. "She is gifted with an ability to step into a room and quickly ascertain where to bring improvement. She has good insight into how to practically apply solutions and bring wholeness into people's hearts. She knows she carries something that adds value and brings positive change to individuals and organizations, and she's not slow in speaking up (not nagging, whining, or negativity). Nor does she easily back down."

Andy understands empowering Janine to be a matter of "recognizing her authority, influence, gifting, and calling, and using my influence to recognize, receive, and release them. Practically, this involves many things, from asking for her input and adjusting accordingly, promoting her when I have opportunities, encouraging her to take opportunities to speak or be influential, and sometimes staying home and caring for our kids so she can go to an event or training." Though he says he has never really felt emasculated or intimidated by her growth as a leader, he was afraid initially that it would pull her away from him and their family. "But when I actually nailed what the fear was," he says, "I realized it was unfounded. I worked through it by talking with spiritual fathers who brought clearer perspective, feeding my intimacy with God, and talking to Janine about my fears. I stayed vulnerable and refused to stop growing in my own relationship with the Father who secures my identity."

Instead of creating disconnection, Andy sees that empowering Janine has strengthened their connections with one another and with their children. "When I empower my wife, she comes to life and thrives, which means that she is happier and we have a happier home. I benefit from the increased intimacy we share when she feels valued and powerful in our marriage. I feel fulfilled, because her success is part of my dream and role as her husband. I also get to hear more and more reports from people saying how their lives have been transformed due to her contact and influence, which spurs me on to run faster and do greater things. I grow personally and end up receiving credit for growth that is really a direct result of listening to my wife."

Andy is candid that the growth he's experienced from leading with Janine hasn't always been comfortable. However, he's grown to love and draw on the productive tension created by calling on her opinions and perspectives, which are often very different than his. "I love her teaching," he says. "She brings a perspective and practical revelation that brings something from the head to the heart. She does the same with me personally when I run ideas past her, whether I'm planning for my own speaking engagements, or facing challenges personally or with people. Often, I don't like her opinions when I first hear them because they are different than mine and require change. Humility is not fun for the male ego. But I have learned that if I will be patient and listen then I will benefit greatly—from the boardroom to the bedroom!"

"My greatness is multiplied as I give my life to help her shine," affirms

Andy. "I am absolutely comfortable when Janine takes center stage and lives are transformed. I love it! That is our call together. It is super fun to see her 'bring it' and sit back and say 'Whose wife is that?' It is super fun to encourage her and see her rise up and become who she was born to be. It's super sexy too! My marriage *is* my ministry. Janine has taught me the priorities of Heaven—the priority of family. I have learned, like Moses, that I would rather die in the desert with these people than get to my 'promise' alone. I am called to walk *with* my wife and family just like God chooses to walk *with* me."

A Pastor, Not Just a Pastor's Wife

It's not always the case that a pastor's wife is gifted and called to lead as a pastor herself, but this is the case with leaders Steve and Wendy Backlund. The Backlunds served for seventeen years as senior pastors for two local churches before coming to work with Global Legacy, the administrative organization that oversees Bethel Church's apostolic network. They are now both authors and travel extensively to teach and advise church leaders.

When they were local church pastors, Steve says, "Wendy preached regularly, contributed strongly in elder meetings, and helped set the course of the church. I have seen firsthand the benefits of a powerful woman in the church world."

However, Wendy's leadership gifts might have remained underdeveloped if Steve had not empowered her to use them early on. "I have to admit that I would never be classified as a powerful woman except for the influence he has had on my life, because I used to be timid and happy in the background," says Wendy. "Between God and my husband's encouragement I feel that my true gifts and callings were able to emerge in a healthy way. He truly desires to see me succeed and encourages me to step out of my comfort zone."

"Wendy is revelation machine," Steve says, "And when she began to emerge as a leader, it was a little intimidating. I was used to getting all the attention, and after a while many people liked her ministry more than mine! I worked through this in two ways: 1) I realized that she carries something I didn't and people needed her, and 2) she is my biggest encourager and constantly tells me that she is what she is because of me." Steve now recognizes that "a powerful, healthy woman is a great reflection on you and will make your life easier and more fruitful."

Wendy affirms this: "As a team we are able to accomplish more with less effort. Just as I benefited from his gifts, he is now benefiting from my gifts. I never sense a competitive spirit on him because he sincerely believes that we are a team."

Steve carries a core value in his ministry and his marriage: "Developing people is more important than my goals or vision." Believing this is what motivates him to empower Wendy by "believing in her and giving her opportunities. I have regularly invited her to minister, influenced her decision-making, and set her up for success by putting good people around her to help her reach her dreams." Steve also protects his wife by "being very watchful of her load-bearing capacity and things or people who threaten her well-being. I encourage her to do things, but also know when to say, 'You need to rest. I will take care of this.'"

"Wendy is very powerful," Steve says. "She is confident in her identity in Christ and as a leader. She does not feel that she has to prove anything to others. She carries a high-level anointing that dramatically impacts both men and women. She is a great leader. People follow her because she speaks their language and they can relate to her. She is where people want to be, so they follow."

Leading in Ministry and the Marketplace

Sadie Hess is the founder of Compass SLS & ILS, a care provider for adults with disabilities now serving three different cities in California. Sadie was already moving with great momentum in her career when her husband, Eric, came into her life. She says that one of the most impressive things about him was that he was not intimidated by her strong personality, ambition, and success. "I knew he was 'the one' when he came to one of my events where I'm powerful and in charge and he was clearly okay with me shining," she says. "We were just friends at the time, and he made sure I had a glass of water and found other ways to help me. That glass of water started a pattern of his willingness to come alongside, help, and be a safe place for me to vent, share, and debrief."

"Another time I knew I'd met the right man for me was when he stood up to me the first time," Sadie continues. "He had inadvertently hurt my feelings and embarrassed me in front of others, but when he realized it, he apologized in front of the group. He looked into my eyes and there was strength there that said, 'I mean my apology, and I expect you to accept it.' I realized that I had met a man who I couldn't manipulate or walk on and dishonor. Most strong women see public expressions of error as weakness, but for Eric, it was his strength on display. When he did that, I knew that I wouldn't escalate things just because I had the power to. His strength enabled me to make better choices."

Eric says that Sadie was exactly the kind of woman he was looking for. "What I appreciate about her strength may be unique to me, but it's that she has *so much*. Before finding my wife, I knew I wanted a woman I would admire and who would contribute in meaningful ways to our marriage and our life. I didn't want a passive wallflower. They may look beautiful in their potted soil, but they don't do much, and they require a lot of tending. I'm just not built for a woman like that, and quite frankly, I find them boring. Instead, I wanted a woman who would bring excitement and adventure to our lives, and who would challenge me to grow into the man God has destined me to be. That is Sadie completely!"

"'Covering' Sadie means a few things," says Eric. "First, it means validating and committing to her dreams as she does to mine. I don't just approve her vision; I let her feel my active support, which gives her a sense of safety and the extra strength she needs to effectively balance work and family. When she feels my strength in situations that challenge her, even if it's just me standing with her, she feels protected and is more able to continue pursuing what she's after. Secondly, my covering gives her a sense of stability, a foundation, to work from. When she has been called upon to speak before large groups, I have observed with joy how my being there—just smiling at her and communicating to her how proud of her I am—allows her to ignore the fear that she's not going to do well, and then just shine. Thirdly, there are occasionally times when her passion can get a bit ahead of her. At those times, I can kind of pull her back from the edge and remind her what is really important at that moment. I have to be careful to maintain honor and respect as I do this, because obviously she will not receive words from a dictator husband. I developed this skill early in our marriage when, like all young couples, we had to work through a few issues. A few times, Sadie would, in hurt and anger, want to shut down. I was able to say, 'Honey, I know this is hard, but we need to work this out, or else our marriage may not become what we want it to be.' Even a woman as powerful and strong as she is listened to me and could follow me instead of her emotions. I don't have to pick up that tool very often, but when I do, she respects it."

"Eric is relentless in his pursuit of connection," Sadie says. "He will not only pursue me to speak my mind, which comes effortlessly, but to speak my heart, which doesn't. There are times when I am shutting down or speaking in anger, and the little girl in me thinks, 'Please, Eric, try one more time.' Invariably he does, and I feel rescued from the tower in which I placed myself. He doesn't let me stay in my hard shell. He makes me break through to the more vulnerable side. Sometimes, I don't know where his sheer will comes from. Nevertheless, I'm grateful, because it's who I want to be, both vulnerable and free."

Eric also values and draws on Sadie's input in his life. "When we were dating, God spoke to me and said, 'Eric, there are some things I will only say to you through her.' I am very grateful to the Lord for that word because I have found her to be full of wisdom and good insight, and I may have been less open to her influence in my life if He hadn't prepared me. I am a speaker and a leader, and when we were first married, submitting to her teaching or influence personally or professionally did make me feel threatened or small," he admits. "What I had to realize is that just because my wife has wisdom and insight which applies to me and *I didn't get that wisdom on my own*, that doesn't mean I'm less worthy of her love and admiration. In fact, by listening to her and receiving from her, I validate her and demonstrate that I value and respect her."

In their early years of marriage, Eric and Sadie had separate careers, but while Sadie's business experienced growth and success, Eric's career experienced setbacks and struggles, which exposed some insecurity in him: "Like most men, I looked at my professional success (or lack thereof) as the wage for my wife's respect. Eventually, I realized that just because she was successful in her career and I was struggling didn't mean I'm not worthy of respect, even from her. The breakthrough for me was the revelation that I am worthy of honor because my Dad says I'm worthy, and her professional success has no bearing on my internal worth or authority.

When I demonstrated to her that even if I had career setbacks or failures, I still expected to be respected, and then managed myself in difficult situations, she felt safe and was able to submit to my spiritual authority in the home."

Eric and Sadie now partner together in business, ministry, and raising their three children. "Today, we have an uncommon life and call in that we do most public work together," Eric says. "We teach and lead teams together. However, I have great appreciation for Sadie's gifts that outshine mine. For example, she is a better visionary and a better problem-solver than I am. This even manifests in our spiritual gifting. She is very prophetic and her anointing is profound. When I make sure she feels safe and protected in an environment, and then come alongside her, literally standing behind her and praying for her, the Holy Spirit will show up and bring amazing revelations through her. It's like my presence behind her takes her up a notch. And then my prophetic will activate, and I will get the interpretation of the word she received, enabling me to assist her by communicating to the person what the Father wants to say. Our team ministry is a blast, and it usually begins with her receiving the word."

"When she's out in front and visible I find her super hot and sexy," Eric adds. "I love it when other people get to see the treasure in her that I see. And it makes me feel pretty good that, well, 'That chick is mine.'"

Leading Separate Ministries

Stephen K. De Silva is the chief financial officer of Bethel Church, the founder of Prosperous Soul, a financial training ministry, and the author of many Prosperous Soul educational resources, including the book *Money and the Prosperous Soul.* Stephen's wife, Dawna, is the co-founder and leader of Bethel Sozo, a deliverance ministry that, since its founding in 1997, has become established in thirty-two states and fifteen countries.

"I have known Dawna since she was eleven years old," says Stephen. "I have seen her rise to the top of every sports team [softball], office staff, and peer group. She is *buoyant* because of her gifting! Dawna is gifted as a leader, and now leads a vast team of self-motivated lay ministers locally, regionally, and internationally. Men and women gladly follow Dawna's leadership, and her effectiveness is clearly demonstrated by the consistent quality of ministry that has flowed through the Transformation Center [Bethel's inner healing and counseling center, where Bethel Sozo is based]. She sees things clearly, naturally makes decisions well, and I especially appreciate her confidence in what she believes. Dawna is wise and anointed. I value her opinion. And she's easy to look at."

Dawna's growth as a leader, which has required an increasingly heavy traveling schedule, initially created a strain in their family. "When Dawna first began to travel, it was very difficult for me," Stephen admits. "Our children were young and their social demands created a profound challenge, especially with my own pressures at work. And Dawna's travel introduced such a stress on what our priorities were at the time. It affected our children and my own energies. But Dawna worked tirelessly to prepare for trips in advance. I watched her efforts to help, and I came to understand that I was as much a part of her travel as she was. She was in the field, but I was enabling her to run. I was her intercessor as well, knowing that her success was, in no small part, a product of my covering, blessing, and prayers. We became a team."

Dawna's growth not only challenged them to develop their teamwork skills as a couple, but also encouraged Stephen to continue growing as a leader himself. "I learned that my insecurities were more about me than her," he says. "She was 'happening,'. And the question the Holy Spirit asked me was, 'So, what are you going to do to happen as well?' While Dawna was gone, I learned to have a life—not to grow apart from her, but to develop and fill my own significance."

Though they as a couple spend considerable amounts of time apart compared to others, Stephen feels very active in empowering, covering, and protecting Dawna. "Empowering my wife is, to me, a matter of *promotion* and *enablement*. By promotion, I mean setting her up for opportunities to grow and succeed. By enablement, I mean kicking down any obstacles, providing help, and sharing the load. It doesn't mean placing her in positions she isn't willing or qualified to be—she must fill her own shoes. But I intentionally and proactively watched our children so she could 'happen,' worked many extra hours to provide money when a nascent Sozo ministry was a financial drain on our family budget, and continue to accept lonely times while she travels. I have also covered her by creating a safe place for her to fail or be weak. Hard times and pressure squeeze the worst out of the best of us. Times have seen Dawna tearful, unsure, or angry. She is a leader and a powerful minister, but she is also a woman. Her times have come when she isn't heroic, and those are the secret times when I am her tender champion. And I have protected her by defending her weak spots. How common it is for lovers to render the most harm, knowing the other's weakness. Protecting Dawna means guarding her flank, even from myself when necessary. It's too easy for others to fling careless criticism; I defend her integrity in those rare times."

Transforming a Nation

Rolland and Heidi Baker founded Iris Ministries as young missionaries and newlyweds in 1980. Today, they stand at the forefront of one of the world's fastest growing revivals, which is bringing restoration and reformation to the nation of Mozambique. Iris has founded and oversees a missions training school, thousands of churches, schools, clinics, orphanages, and many community projects such as well-drilling. A passionate preacher with a knack for languages, Heidi has naturally assumed the more visible role in leading the ministry and now maintains an extremely busy schedule, teaching both in the bush and internationally at churches, ministry schools, and conferences.

"Heidi has been a strong, tenacious, independent leader with great initiative since she was very young," says Rolland. "Her mother describes her ordering classmates around in her schoolyard organizing games. She thrived being away from home as a foreign exchange student, pursuing many interests. Once filled with the Spirit and told to be a minister, she preached to whomever would listen, even though in her environment she had never heard of women preachers. After being healed of severe dyslexia, she learned championship speed reading so she could spend more time in ministry while in college. She took two years of classes in one to get to the mission field faster. She was obedient to Go,d whatever the cost, and was fearless about living by faith. She was given a mandate by God to be a minister and missionary to Asia, England, and Africa, and she has never looked back, no matter the obstacles and criticism. In Mozambique, women are rarely in Church leadership, but even the strongest men, including ex-military officers who were responsible for killing thousands of people during Mozambique's wars, gladly follow Heidi's leadership to the letter. I ask Mozambican pastors, 'Do you accept women in leadership in your culture?' They say, 'No.' I then ask, 'What about Heidi?' They say, 'Oh, she's different. We know she loves us!' She is able to be strong, and yet loving and feminine to the nth degree—a magnificent achievement."

When I asked Rolland about what it looks like to "empower" and "cover" Heidi, he said, "Heidi doesn't need any special 'covering' or 'protection' apart from simple, normal love that does that anyway. Our marriage and ministry are never in competition, and we both are empowered to the max just as Jesus desires through our various gifts and emphases. God evens everything out, and we are both fully aware of how much we need each other."

"We have agreed not to make a major decision without agreement, and I get no pleasure from overriding her," he continues. "Heidi is one of the very few prophetic voices that I trust almost completely. She follows Jesus in a pure-hearted, naïve, childlike way free from ambitious agendas, and she almost never misses or claims to know the voice of the Lord when she doesn't. The fruit of her obedience confirms her experiences with God and the direction she gets. So I respect her and listen to her like I do any pure child of God, male or female. I have nothing to gain by not doing so."

Women in Leadership

I asked all these men to weigh in on what they, as partners of women leaders, thought about women leading in the Church. Unsurprisingly, they all agreed that qualified women could and should lead, and that the Body of Christ can only gain by receiving the gifts God has given them.

"Of course [called and gifted women should lead]," said Rolland. "They are God's choice, and not because men defaulted to them. The Church is receiving progressive revelation through history toward 'neither male nor female.' That she is a woman is beside the point. God in her is the value! Let the power of God settle the issue. It's all about love and selflessness."

Stephen said, "Gender brings different expressions to power and influence like color brings variety to a flower garden. But I easily and comfortably perceive women as equals. I cannot imagine a woman as being anything but equal, and I don't tolerate a backward opinion of the inferiority of either sex. I believe every leader faces challenges of character, like honesty and integrity, but none of those virtues are a possession of gender."

"The question of female equality feels like an issue answered many years past," Stephen continues. "Frankly, it tires me to hear the continuing discussion of the message because it falls *behind* me, not ahead of me. Of course, I understand this discussion remains necessary for many men and women. But this whole topic feels like an echo from the past, like the flat earth theory, and represents a sad commentary that followers of Christ are mired in a problem where they should be leading."

"When Paul wrote, 'There is neither male, nor female' he either meant it or he didn't," says Eric. "While I do think that in the family there is structure that God designed, I don't think that God ever meant that women weren't meant to have authority over men outside the family. This is an area in which the Church is way behind the 'world.' At nearly all levels of society—Fortune 500 companies, politics, education, etc.—women have demonstrated that they can carry as much authority and be as effective as men. The ability to lead people well or achieve positive results is not bound by gender in the marketplace, so why would God put that kind of boundary on His part of the marketplace, His Church?"

"Unless you sit under powerful women, you are only getting half of the message," Steve Backlund says simply. "Women process things differently, and we need their perspective."

Skyler agrees. 'If you sit under men your whole life, you're obviously going to get a similar perspective on certain issues all the time," he says. "If you sit under a woman in that situation, you'll get a different perspective. There's tons of benefits in having multiple perspectives from which you can gain wisdom and develop your own opinion. Why would you not want to diversify and gain that wisdom?"

Andy Mason also affirms that when you have women on your leadership team, "You gain a perspective you would never have from men alone and a greater measure of relational influence and capacity—for example, the compassion, nurture, and heart stuff that most guys are missing. You'll receive a challenge to go further, influence wider, and love deeper. And you'll develop connection with the whole (individual or corporate) rather than focus on a certain compartment or single area."

From Strength to Strength

In the next chapter, we will explore some of the practical ways we as the Body can begin to empower the women of God in our marriages and churches. But in closing, I want to leave you—particularly you men—with some final words of encouragement from these Proverbs 31 men.

"If you're not in relationship with a powerful woman, have some courage and go for it," Skyler says. "She's going to stretch you and cause you to become a better leader and a more powerful man yourself. It's going to cause you to learn how to communicate and deal with powerful people. It will cause you to grow on multiple levels."

In a marriage with a strong woman, Andy says, "You will develop a deeper connection and relationship—greater intimacy. The benefits to a man's sex life are always a great motivator! You'll be happier, more creative, more expressive. You get to see someone become who they were born to be, which is exhilarating! You get shaped into something far more than if you had been in relationship with a doormat, 'yes' woman, or powerless creature."

Stephen agrees: "Being married to a powerful woman doesn't demean you; it expands you. Expect to be challenged, and prepare to grow to keep up. I believe a couple can only go as high, metaphorically speaking, as the lowest partner's ceiling. God holds our sky open, if we are willing to grow as individuals and as a couple. Get a vision!"

Steve Backlund says, "Celebrate your powerful woman, become her biggest cheerleader, and then get ready for the ride of your life! Pursue radical growth and thrive in what makes you come alive in life or ministry." Rolland echoes this admonition to men: "Rejoice in her, and look forward to all that God will do through you, as well, at the right time!"

Chapter Eight

⸻ ❧❦❧ ⸻

PERMISSION TO BE
POWERFUL

The enemy has always had a special hatred of women—ever since God prophesied that a woman would play a key role in defeating him: *"I will put enmity between you and the woman, and between your seed and her Seed; He shall bruise your head, and you shall bruise His heel"* (Gen. 3:15). Because God chose a woman to bring the Redeemer into the world, the devil declared war on women. At a spiritual level, this is why we have a history full of underdeveloped and abused women. The devil has worked very hard to convince men that women are to be feared and suppressed. Frankly, he has done a great job throughout history of recruiting men to keep his war on women going strong.

Yet, despite his vicious and relentless campaign, the enemy could not stop the prophecy from coming true. Mary received the word of the angel Gabriel that she would conceive through the seed of God and became pregnant (see Luke 1:26-38). God deposited the solution to humanity's hopelessness, the Champion who would finally vanquish the deceiver and end his war, within a woman—without a man's involvement.

It's easy for us to miss it, because we know the end of the story, but this was a very sobering revelation for Mary. It undermined everything she had been taught by the religious system and the patriarchal paradigm. She knew the consequences could be disastrous. The law commanded that anyone who committed adultery be put to death (see Lev. 20:10). Mary knew she would be perceived as an adulteress. No other virgin had ever supernaturally conceived a child from Heaven. When Mary said yes to God's plan, she stepped into a position of ridicule, ostracism, and very real danger.

Significantly, Mary's name, which comes from the Hebrew *Miryam*, means "their rebellion."[1] By carrying the seed of God, Mary became a symbol of rebellion in her culture. And though Mary became pregnant without a man, she *did* need a man's help confronting one of the most rigid cultural systems on the planet. She needed a partner who would shield and protect her as God's plan came to fruition.

In order to be the man Mary needed, Joseph had to believe in her. He had to believe in God—who thankfully sent him an angel, too, or he might never have believed Mary (see Matt. 1:18-25). He had to bear the brunt of the cultural stigma for marrying an unchaste woman and overcome his own ingrained cultural training. And he did it. Joseph defied his culture right along with Mary. He married her and stood between her and the fear, danger, and condemnation. He even put away his right to be intimate with his virgin bride in order to protect what God was doing through her. Joseph was a truly faithful and courageous man!

Together, Mary and Joseph protected the seed of God in Mary's womb and enabled His solution for humanity's problems to enter a hostile environment. As a team, they became hosts of God's presence in a way that forever changed the world. Considering the original design of creation, it is no surprise that God used a man and woman walking in oneness with Him and one another to bring His plan for redemption into the world.

What happened with Mary and Joseph was only the beginning. I believe women still play a special role in God's redemptive plan. Our male-dominated, patriarcha paradigml–oriented world needs the seed of God hidden in women. He is looking for women who defy cultural norms and restrictions in order to bring forth something that will change a generation. He is looking for women who refuse to listen to tradition and fearlessly pursue obedience to the call of God on their lives. But women cannot step into this freedom and power on their own. They need faithful men to walk with them and empower them to step into their destiny in the midst of the storms of culturally ingrained opposition.

Some women hate the idea of needing help from a man, but this is just as wrong as men hating the idea of needing help from a woman. God created us to need each other. As much as men need to value what women bring to the table, women also need to value help from men as they step into places of power and influence. It takes Josephs to have Marys. If Mary had not had Joseph, she would have been killed or hidden far away in the desert. Her community would have rejected her as a law-breaker and a rebel. If Joseph hadn't come along and stepped in to protect her, we wouldn't have Jesus or freedom in the earth. God knew what He was doing when He brought Mary and Joseph together as a team.

Neither men nor women can do this on their own. *We need each other.* In order to bring Heaven to earth and accurately represent Jesus to the world, we need to restore the unity that God has intended for us from the beginning. We need to live and love as individuals who know we are stronger when we're together. When we do, it will be the beginning of something big, something truly remarkable. I believe the Lord has a surprise attack for the enemy that comes on the other side of Joseph protecting Mary. Male-female partnerships are about to unleash a secret weapon on the earth.

Becoming Emancipators

The men and women you heard from in the last chapter are powerful forerunners for male-female partnerships. They are also the exception—by far—in the Body of Christ. A very real power difference exists between men and women in the Church today. We no longer argue over whether there's a fundamental difference in value or innate capabilities between whites and blacks or between rich and poor. (Certainly, in some environments, a division of classes and races still exists, but it's no longer acceptable to debate the value of one of these groups over the other.) However, the oppression of women is not only still acceptable, but it is also openly taught and ardently protected within a very large section of the Body of Christ.

Only a few years ago, in 2009, former United States President Jimmy Carter left his church denomination of over sixty years because of his disgust with their view of women. He called his decision unavoidable after the leaders prohibited women from being ordained and insisted that women be subservient to their husbands. He had tried to influence the denomination to change their policies, but to no effect. He wrote:

> At its most repugnant, the belief that women must be subjugated to the wishes of men excuses slavery, violence, forced prostitution, genital mutilation and national laws that omit rape as a crime. But it also costs many millions of girls and women control over their own bodies and lives, and continues to deny them fair access to education, health, employment and influence within their own communities.

He went on to say:

> The truth is that male religious leaders have had—and still have— an option to interpret holy teachings either to exalt or subjugate women. They have, for their own selfish ends, overwhelmingly chosen the latter. Their continuing choice provides the foundation or justification for much of the pervasive persecution and abuse of women throughout the world. [2]

I agree with Jimmy Carter. This *is* a pressing issue of justice today, and we men have a choice. Either we can embrace the Gospel of freedom and empower women, or we can use the Scriptures to empower our fears and oppress women. Do we want to lead the charge or follow along at the rear? I want to lead the charge. Hopefully you're with me. Nevertheless, I fully appreciate the fact that most male leaders don't know where to begin in the project of emancipating women in the Church.

Incidentally, the man who became our Great Emancipator, Abraham Lincoln, began his presidency without a strategy for emancipating slaves. I believe the events that unfolded to give him a strategy can provide us with a key for developing our own.[3] Lincoln came into office as a great politician who was actually trying to figure out a way to protect slavery in the South— if it would preserve the union of the nation. Lincoln knew slavery was an injustice, and he didn't want it to spread to other regions of the nation. But he feared that outlawing it altogether would cause the nation to split. So he created a law that prohibited the new western territories from having slaves, and that preserved freedom in the North and slavery in the South. If a slave ran away and was caught in the North, the slave would be sent back to the master in the South. The government could not interfere with someone's personal property. Its job was to protect property owners, and this included slave owners because slaves were considered property. As the steward of that government, Lincoln even argued with his abolitionist cabinet. He insisted on sending slaves back into oppression because his highest priority was to protect the union and the law of the land. He was trying to create a balance that appeased everyone, but it wasn't working.

This is not the side of Abraham Lincoln we normally hear about, but it's history. Abraham Lincoln worked hard to protect the institution of slavery, even though he believed it was wrong, because he wanted to protect the union of the nation. Something had to change in Lincoln to make him the man we know now, and that change came through a relationship with a black man named Frederick Douglass. Before Lincoln met Douglass, he had absolutely no hope that black men could integrate into white society. Given the impoverished and uneducated condition in which slaves had lived for generations, he didn't believe they could ever compete for jobs or function in the economy. His only solution was to ship freed slaves back to Africa or Cuba or South America. Then Lincoln encountered something he did not know existed: an educated and powerful black man.

In that season of national tumult, Douglass became a counselor and friend to the president, and he introduced him to a new way of thinking. At his core, Lincoln believed that all people deserved honor, opportunity, and hope. Frederick Douglass even said, "Abraham Lincoln is the first powerful man who I was in the presence of and didn't feel black."[4] However, Lincoln operated in a government that wouldn't allow him to express these beliefs. Then suddenly he found himself partnered with this educated black man who, through extraordinary opportunities and connections, had risen above the norm of his day. Lincoln began thinking very differently when he saw what a former slave could become. Instead of shipping the former slaves to Africa, he started imagining how they could be integrated into American society.

One of the biggest shifts in Lincoln's thinking came when Douglass challenged him to allow freed black men to prove their patriotism and serve as soldiers in the Union Army. The politicians were afraid that freed men would use their new power to kill their former oppressors. Though they believed black people should be free, they still weren't sure black people could be trusted to be noble. They suggested that the black men be drafted into the army but not given weapons. Fortunately, through his relationship with Frederick Douglass, Lincoln realized that freedom isn't freedom if it doesn't come with power. In order for these black men to fully be men, they needed to be just as powerful as white men. He championed the idea, though many fought him because they were afraid of powerful black people. Eventually they were persuaded when they realized that arming black soldiers would effectively reduce the South's resources and increase the North's chances of winning the war. Lincoln's faith was rewarded as his black soldiers demonstrated their commitment to serve honorably and give their lives for their country, and they earned great respect throughout the remainder of the war.

When Abraham Lincoln gave weapons to black soldiers, he gave them permission to be powerful. He invited them to fight for the same cause with the same tools and the same dignity as the white men. This is our formula for emancipation. Like Lincoln did in his day, we recognize that the current inequality in the Church is wrong. We want change; we want to see the women empowered. Yet if we're honest, many of us men also fear the idea of giving women real power. It feels like giving guns to former slaves. Like Lincoln, we must recognize that freedom isn't freedom without power. Women will never be equal with men as long as their access to power is restricted. When we see this, we will also see that—as with the Union Army and its black soldiers—the key to victory in our war against evil is to empower women.

Learning to Be Powerful

In addition to giving women power, we need to replace their powerless paradigm with an empowered paradigm, and give women skills to use their power well. We also need to understand that this is not something that happens overnight and requires sustained resistance to cultural pressure. Abraham Lincoln signed the Emancipation Proclamation in 1863. A century later, in 1963, Martin Luther King Jr. delivered his famous "I Have a Dream" speech and led the charge for racial equality and the end to discrimination in America. It took one hundred years to sufficiently unravel the fabric of oppression—which was ingrained in the oppressed as much as in the oppressors—so that a majority of people could agree that the color of a person's skin didn't define that person's worth. A little over fifty years later, in 2008, a black man was elected president of the United States. It took 150 years for our nation to make the transition from property to president. I am working hard to make sure it won't take that long for women in the Church.

Though women in the Church have not experienced the sort of oppression and abuse that slaves did (at least not in this nation), they have still grown up in a paradigm that has not equipped them practically for leadership or positions of power. We have centuries of stop signs for women that need to be pulled out so they can learn to run alongside the men, share the same opportunities for training in leadership, and most importantly, establish the same belief in their self-worth and abilities. I'm not saying that all women should be in leadership any more than I'm saying all men should. Those who are gifted in leadership should be in leadership. And in order for them to be successful, they need to be developed as leaders and given experience.

Men and women need to be given the same opportunities for development so that when it is game time, the women are prepared to perform as well as the men. Unfortunately, in their desire to promote women, I have seen some churches rush the process and promote women who haven't been sufficiently trained. Then, when these ladies can't handle the pressure or just don't have the needed skills, it is seen as a failure of women rather than a failure in training. This doesn't help anyone. If we really believe in empowering our women, we need to give them access to the same training and practical experience that men receive on their journey toward leadership.

The Nuances of Oppression

After giving our women power and the tools to use it well, we must be sure to uncover and address the nuances of oppression that still exist in our church cultures. This is difficult because, by definition, nuances are subtle. They are the outworking of our subconscious opinions about women. In order to remove these nuances, we need to change our hearts. If we don't, we will inevitably be ruled by our inner paradigm, regardless of what we're telling other people we believe about women in leadership.

One common nuance I have observed is the quiet relegation of women to women's ministry. We think women will feel empowered if we put them in their own little group with their own little government and events and say, "Hey, you ladies are free." That's normal in many churches, but that's *not* freedom. That's like Abraham Lincoln thinking the solution to slavery was sending the freed slaves to create their own little society in Cuba. We didn't send freed slaves to Cuba, but we did create a little Cuba for them right here at home in the States called Segregation. It didn't work. "Separate but equal" is a logical contradiction. Equality is expressed through partnership. Our women love the Church and want to be part of it. They do not want to be relegated to a side group. They want to be part of the big picture, part of the union. They want to run as equals with the men.

This generation of women is asking for permission to be just as powerful as everyone else. They are looking for people who will give them that permission. In order to answer that call, we need to honestly examine our lives. First, we need to ask God for revelation and a changed heart. Second, as we learned from Lincoln and Douglass, we need to actively seek positive experiences and relationships with powerful women who can open our imaginations and hearts to receive them in our circles of influence. The biographies of transformational women in history, particularly Church history, are a good place to start. Lastly, as scary or painful as it may be, we need to ask the women we know to help us see the truth about how we think and act toward them. If we don't, our wives and our daughters will have a very hard time experiencing the freedom and power they were made for.

Some men, when they hear others talk about the oppression of women in the Church, think, *My wife doesn't feel that way.* But how can we know unless we ask them? How can we know unless we give them the opportunity to tell us the truth? If my wife knows that I will be grumpy and refuse to talk to her for days after she confronts an issue in my life, she may decide to just keep her mouth shut. Many women have learned that telling their husbands how they really feel is like inviting a bulldozer to overrun their Mini Cooper.

It takes great courage to decide, "This little pet oppression of mine will no longer live in peace. I will fight it until it leaves because it is hurting the people I love!" As men, we must rise to that challenge. We must become champions of freedom for all. If we truly want Heaven's government to be established as the foundation for our lives, we must boldly face this question: *What will we do with the nuances of oppression in our lives that hold back the Kingdom of Heaven from being established on the earth?*

Practical Steps

My goal in *Powerful and Free* is not to put forth some kind of political plan for achieving gender equality in the Church. Even the best-laid plans will fail if we do not deal with the infection of patriarchy in the root system of our hearts. The only way to deal with that infection is to see and receive something better—the Kingdom. Jesus' upside-down Kingdom is the only thing that will satisfy the deep longing for power, freedom, and equality at our core. This is why Jesus taught that the most practical thing in the Christian life is simply to go after the Kingdom with everything in us (see Matt. 6:33).

In the Kingdom, we never solve problems through legalism. Every problem is solved through relationship. Political institutions are limited to legalistic machinery when they solve problems, and unfortunately, legalism and mature human relationships are fundamentally at odds. God designed relationships to flow from the internal law of love that He alone can write on our hearts. External laws inherently conflict with this internal freedom. This is why legalistic strategies to achieve equality, like segregation or affirmative action, may eliminate certain problems, but end up causing a bunch of other problems. Telling businesses and universities that they must include people for the same reason they were formerly excluded (race or gender) may open the door to some people who genuinely deserve those opportunities. But it never deals with the fear that caused us to give or take value from those people in the first place. A law forcing the redistribution of privileges cannot create value for another human being in our hearts. But that is the best the world can do. Only the Gospel of eternal, equal value creates a new paradigm where we can freely honor and partner with one another as equals. That said, I do want to present you with a few practical steps for pursuing a Kingdom-driven shift in our gender paradigm.

1. Know What the Bible Says

Most of the Christians working hard to protect the oppression of women in the Church have well-researched Scriptural arguments backed by centuries of tradition to support their position. They are driven to support their beliefs at all cost. It can be tempting for those of us who believe women should be free to simply ignore those troublesome passages. We know these interpretations can't be right, but we haven't taken the time to dig and figure out why we believe what we believe. This allows room for complacency and even doubt, thus undermining our confidence and impacting the way we treat women. We need to study the Bible to find freedom for our women. When we don't know what to do with certain passages, we need to get help from the theologians. I'm not saying we can figure it all out. There will always be some mystery. But what we can do is discover the overwhelming evidence in Scripture that God wants women to be powerful and free right alongside the men.

2. Teach Our Friends

Once we study it for ourselves, we will be able to teach others what Scripture says about empowering women. This isn't just the job of the preachers and teachers. It's the job of *every* believer, because freedom is the Gospel message. If we want this idea to really take root in the Church and change the way we do things, it needs to become part of our conversations—not just among the leaders, but among everyone. We need to tell our friends what we think about women, and we need to be ready to explain what the Bible actually says on the subject.

3. Talk to Women

Hearing women's stories and feeling a piece of their pain will open our eyes to the need for change. We need to talk to some of the women we know and ask them how it feels to be a woman in Christian culture. We need to find the ones who felt called to be apostolic or prophetic leaders in the Church, but instead had to start a business or work in government in order to be free of the restrictions the Church placed on them. It may take some time before they trust us enough to tell the truth, but we must persist until we hear it.

4. Eliminate Sexist Humor

Men tend to communicate through humor more than women do. Many are unaware of the ways in which their humor alienates the women in their environment. Obviously, sexist jokes—including blonde jokes and jokes about female stereotypes—need to be eliminated in order to make an environment safe for women. On a more subtle level, male humor can also be used to make women feel like "one of the guys." However, most women do not want to be "one of the guys." They aren't men, and they don't want to be treated as men. They want the same respect and equality men receive, but with regard for who they are as women. For too long, women have had to become "one of the guys" in order to have any place in the male-dominated leadership realms. We will know we've reached equality when women receive equal power and respect without needing to curb their femininity.

5. Value and Seek Out Opinions from Women

The opinions of women are not as valued as opinions of men in the male-dominated environment of most churches. Men tend to seek out other men for advice first, and they often assume that women will not have much to offer—especially to them. A subconscious attitude exists in many men that women are good at advising other women, but that their advice would not be good enough for the men. We would not say this, of course, but many of us think it. If we truly want to empower women, we need to begin valuing their opinions—which means actively seeking them out.

6. Deliberately Remove Obstacles to Women Holding Ministry Positions

Because churches and Christian organizations hold nonprofit status with the government, they are not required by law to provide paid maternity leave to their employees. And most churches don't. Though this may seem like a small thing, it reveals our beliefs about the importance of having women on staff. A friend of mine recently told me how the example of her mother, who worked as a teacher all through her growing up years, empowered her to go for her dreams. She said, "I got to watch my mom perform this dance of being an excellent mom and a professional in the workplace. Nothing felt neglected, and it gave me vision that I could do whatever I wanted as a woman. There was no polarization between motherhood and career." This friend suggested, "The Church should make it easy for women to work while being mothers. We need to change the way we think about what women do. What kind of influence can we really have if all of the women are relegated to the family and no other dimension of society?"

I couldn't agree more. If we really believe we need women on our team, we will do all we can to remove the obstacles that make it difficult for mothers to work for churches and ministries. We will provide paid maternity leave and pursue creative solutions, like job sharing, for mothers who want to work part-time.[5]

7. Put Women Up Front

As children grow, they watch and learn what it means to act appropriately in their environment from role models. In the Church, for the most part, little girls grow up seeing women work behind the scenes in the nursery, the children's ministry, or administration. Often they see women on the worship team on a Sunday morning. But when it's time for the preaching, they see men. When it's time for decision-making, they see men. And subconsciously they learn that women in the Church are not as powerful as men in the Church. Simply saying that women are powerful will not counteract the message we're communicating to our daughters (and sons) through the lack of powerful female role models. We need to make sure we have visible models of what it looks like for a woman to have authority in the Church. This is the only way our daughters will grow up really believing they are just as free as the men.

8. Empower Women in the Local Church

A core principle of the Kingdom is that all believers are ministers, no matter their vocation. We need both men and women to change the world through positions of influence. Many women are already doing this because it's easier for them to be empowered in the world than in the Church. However, we also need women leading within the Church. Apart from a short list of notable exceptions, like Aimee Semple McPherson, we have only championed powerful women in foreign missions or itinerant ministries—women outside the authority structure of the local church or larger networks and denominations. We can name a handful of powerful women who have parachurch teaching ministries, like Joyce Meyer, Beth Moore, and Cindy Jacobs (who, it must be noted, draw largely female audiences). But where are the female apostolic leaders in America who are leading congregations, denominations, or church networks and are recognized in a positive light rather than being perceived as being suspicious or rebellious? Where are the apostolic women in the Church who are not being persecuted for violating the patriarchal paradigm's longstanding traditions? We need to invite women into the authority structure of the local church alongside men, and not just send them off to be powerful outside the local church. Parachurch ministries are important, but the local church is the center of Church life. We need to give female leaders access to *all levels* of responsibility and authority in the Body of Christ—including the sacred "senior pastor" position. When we do this, it will be proof that we have stopped dividing up authority based on gender. It will be proof that we've begun to truly honor women.

The Meaning of Honor

When we share power, we elevate the status of another. That is the definition of *honor*. Sometimes we think of *honor* as "I surrender to you." That sort of honor is really a manifestation of fear. Honor isn't primarily what we give to Billy Graham or to other strangers. Honor is what we give to the members of our household. Honor is tested in our most intimate relationships. Honor happens when we live together, believe together, pray together, fail together, and win together.

Truly empowering other people means allowing them to stay powerful even when we disagree with them and even when they fail. This is what will take us into a new government based on Heaven's model. Honor is the only environment where freedom and love thrive. Without honor, we need legalism and external threats (police, the IRS, courts, and prisons). Without honor, we need someone to be angry at people in order to keep them in their place. But when we have honor, we can confront each other and give healthy feedback on how we're affecting one another without calling for backup. And our motive for confrontation is not because our power feels threatened, but because we have placed a priority on regular relationship maintenance. We expect more from each other.

Honor-based relationships are the only way for men and women to work together with equality and unity. That's the model we see in the Trinity, and it's the answer to Jesus' prayer for unity, *"...that they may be one as We are"* (John 17:11). Honor is the goal, because freedom for everyone can't exist without honor. Church history has proven that. We've had freedom for some and subservience for others for a long time. But if we want a heavenly invasion of earth, we need to change that.

The transition into honor-based relationships needs to be intentional. We're not going to wake up one day and realize we accidentally started honoring women in the Church. This is a transition that needs to be welcomed and pursued, even though it is scary. We've listened to our fears for too long, and it has only brought out the worst in us. It's time to listen to the One who came to free us from our fears and let His love bring out the best in us.

Greatness shows up when it's our turn to stand for something. Right now, it's our turn. We have an opportunity for greatness. Let's become emancipators in our day. Let's become champions of freedom for all—like Paul, who fought for the truth that *"...you are all one in Christ Jesus"* (Gal. 3:28). For too long, men have protected a government that restricts women's power.

It is time for a change.

It is time for us to give weapons to the women.

It is time that we welcome them, as equals, into the great battle to bring Heaven to earth.

HOPE DEFERRED: A NOTE TO THE WOMEN

By Sheri Silk

In Proverbs, it says, *"Hope deferred makes the heart sick…"* (Prov. 13:12). Most of us interpret it like this, "I had a hope, but I didn't get it, which made me sick inside." I believe a better way to read this would be, "I stopped hoping, and *that* is what made me sick." It is the decision to give up on hope that makes our hearts sick.

I have always loved horses, and as a child, I had my own horse. I had mixed experiences with horses—both good and bad. With my own horse, I had lots of fun, but I also was bucked off several times, and once I even broke my arm. One of my close friends was bucked off of a horse, got kicked on her way down, and died as a result.

As an adult, I have always said that I wanted to live next door to horses, because they are fun to watch. But I didn't want to own one. One day, as I was thinking about my call as a woman in leadership, the Lord brought my love of horses to mind. When I asked Him what it meant, He spoke to me, "It's easier to watch power than to walk in it." Then He brought to mind different women I have known who have been bucked off and injured in their attempts to "ride the horse," or to live as *powerful women*. Danny and I know powerful women who don't go to church anymore. The Church didn't value who God created them to be, but shut them down, sometimes in very hurtful ways. Because of their hurt, these women stopped hoping, and that made them heartsick; they simply gave up on the Church.

The remainder of Proverbs 13:12 says, *"...desire fulfilled is a tree of life"* (NASB). That is what we women want—life. We want the freedom to live out who we are in the Kingdom. Yet because of the patriarchal paradigm and all the wrong teaching about women in the Church, many of us have simply accepted the way things are. Some women have left, while others have quietly resigned. Most of us are not the sort who will force our way into power. Either we will adapt to the expectations within the Church, or we will go into the secular workforce to find a place where we can be powerful. We are not rebels at heart, and we need permission to be powerful in the Church. We need men who will promote us, believe in us, and defend us in our culture.

Yet it is also true that the liberation of women in the Church is not dependent on the men changing any more than the Civil Rights movement was dependent on white people leading the charge. No, it was dependent on brave people like Rosa Parks who were not afraid to step outside of the system of oppression and step into their identity as powerful people— even if they didn't yet have permission from the patriarchy. The reason Martin Luther King, Jr.'s ministry had such great impact was because he and his followers found a way to step into their identity as powerful and free people without stepping into rebellion or hatred along the way. I believe we, as women in the Church, can take the same road to empowerment, but it will require great courage.

Proverbs 28:1 tells us that *"...the righteous are bold as a lion."* On the day of Pentecost, when the Holy Spirit invaded the earth, one of the most remarkable evidences of the infilling of the Spirit was boldness. The disciples transitioned, in a moment, from cowards hiding in their homes to bold, powerful, and courageous apostles who would not stop telling the truth for anything. The Church as a whole is at least fifty percent lionesses—and it is time for the lionesses to be powerful and free. It is time for us to expect no limitations and no gender biases. It is time for us to refuse to accept prejudices and to confront them when they arise. It is time for us to have a plan for how to respond to the walls of limitation that we most certainly will run into.

Ladies, we are one hundred percent a "new creation," and we are one hundred percent filled with the Holy Spirit. That means we have the same newness and the same fullness as men. So this question remains:

"What are we going to do with ourselves?"

Now that we know who we are and what we are destined for, we cannot simply sit back and do nothing. We must be who we are called to be. Like the apostles Peter and John, we must declare, *"Whether it is right in the sight of God to listen to you* [the Pharisees, the defenders of tradition] *more than to God, you judge. For we cannot but speak the things which we have seen and heard"* (Acts 4:19-20). We are compelled to enter into the freedom that Jesus purchased for us.

The decision to become powerful women in the Church requires great courage and great commitment to the big picture because we will be the first wave on the shore. Some of us, like the great liberators of history, may suffer for our stance. Yet we have the hope of liberation, not only for ourselves, but also for our daughters. We have the hope that men and women will step into the unity that Jesus prophesied and together establish the Kingdom of Heaven on earth. *"Let us hold fast the confession of our hope without wavering, for He who promised is faithful"* (Heb. 10:23). Hope is a courageous choice—let's chose to never stop hoping.

Recommended Reading

CHRISTIAN SOURCES

Why Not Women? by Loren Cunningham and David Joel Hamilton

10 Lies the Church Tells Women by J. Lee Grady

Women in the Church by Stanley J. Grenz and Denise Muir Kjesbo

The Hidden Power of a Woman by Bonnie and Mahesh Chavda

Beyond Sex Roles by Gilbert Bilezikian

Discovering Biblical Equality edited by Ronald W. Pierce, Rebecca Merrill Groothuis, and Gordon D. Fee

In the Spirit We're Equal by Susan C. Hyatt

Normal Christianity, Chapter 7: "Women Rising" by Jonathan Welton

Christians for Biblical Equality, www.cbeinternational.org

SECULAR SOURCES

Why Women Should Rule the World by Dee Dee Myers

Man Down by Dan Abrams

Endnotes

OPENING QUOTE

1. Rena Pederson, "Paul Praises a Woman Apostle," *E-Quality* 7.1; www.cbeinternational. org/files/u1/free-art/paul-praises-woman-apostle.pdf (accessed June 27, 2012).

CHAPTER 1: THE STORY BEHIND POWERFUL AND FREE

1. For more on Sozo, visit www.bethelsozo.com.

2. I address other aspects of Church culture in my books *Loving Our Kids on Purpose* and *A Culture of Honor*.

3. James W. Goll, "Declarations for 2009 and Beyond," *Encounters Network*; www.encountersnetwork.com/email_blasts/feb_2009_declarations.htm (accessed May 29, 2012).

CHAPTER 2: KNOW THY PLACE

1. Malcolm Gladwell, *Blink* (New York, NY: Hachette Book Group, 2005), 77-88.

2. Gladwell, 85.

3. Loren Cunningham and David Joel Hamilton, with Janice Rogers, *Why Not Women?* (Seattle, WA: Youth With A Mission Publishing, 2000), 77.

4. Cunningham, Hamilton, 77.

5. J. Lee Grady, *10 Lies the Church Tells Women* (Lake Mary, FL: Charisma House, 2000), 18.

6. Grady, 68.

7. Grady, 152.

8. Grady, 18.

9. Cunningham, Hamilton, 97.

10. Dr. Susan C. Hyatt, "Jesus, Friend of Women," GodsWordtoWomen.org (http://godswordtowomen.org/jesus.htm, Accessed September 11, 2012).

11. Cunningham, Hamilton, 119-125.

12. Hyatt, ibid.

13. Cunningham, Hamilton, 121-122.

14. See Tim Keller's book *King's Cross* (an excerpt may be found here: http://www.relevantmagazine.com/god/deeper-walk/features/25243-a-case-for-resurrection) and N.T. Wright's *The Resurrection of the Son of God* for discussions on the significance of the testimony of women in proving the resurrection.

CHAPTER 3: THE REALITY OF THE GLASS CEILING

1. *Merriam Webster's Dictionary.*

2. I have changed their names for their own protection.

3. *Collins English Dictionary,* s.v. "voiceless"; http://www.thefreedictionary.com/voiceless (accessed June 15, 2012).

CHAPTER 4: PAUL: APOSTLE OF FREEDOM AND EQUALITY

1. Chuck Colson, "Domestic Violence within the Church: The Ugly Truth," *Religion Today* (October 20, 2009); http://www.religiontoday.com/news/domestic-violence-within-the-church-the-ugly-truth-11602500.html (accessed June 20, 2012). See also Marcia Ford, "Domestic Violence and the Church," *Spirit-Led Woman* (September 30, 2000); www.charismamag.com/index.php/spiritled-woman/relationships/26873-domestic-violence-and-the-church.

2. "Subjugation of Muslim Women," *Youtube.com;* http://www.youtube.com/watch?v=mzifXKc7mAI (accessed July 9, 2012).

3. If you become aware of physical abuse in your church, or elsewhere—there is only one course of action: *call the police immediately.* Your church has no authority to govern someone who breaks civil law, and it is breaking civil law when you are violent toward another human being. When you try to deal with abuse "in house," you are perpetuating dysfunction in the family and acting outside your authority. The civil court has authority over the abuser; the church does not. The abuser could leave the church, but he cannot leave the court. The court requires the issue be addressed and fixed.

4. Cunningham, Hamilton, 147.

5. see Romans 16:1-2; Cunningham, Hamilton, 149-152.

6. Cunningham, Hamilton, 149.

7. Allison Young, "1 Corinthians 14:34-35," *Christians for Biblical Equality International;* www.cbeinternational.org/?q=content/1-corinthians-1434-35 (accessed May 17, 2012).

8. Cunningham, Hamilton, 190-191. Also see Grady, 62-64.

9. Cunningham, Hamilton, 190.

10. Cunningham, Hamilton, 190.

11. Jonathan Welton, *Normal Christianity* (Shippensburg, PA: Destiny Image 2011), 136-139; Gilbert Bilezikian, *Beyond Sex Roles* (Grand Rapids, MI: Baker, 1986), 144-153.

12. Welton, 132-134; Grady, 57.

13. Sharon Hodgin Gritz, *Paul, Women Teachers and the Mother Goddess at Ephesus: A Study of 1 Timothy 2:9-15 in Light of the Religious and Cultural Milieu of the First Century* (University Press of America, 1991), 31-41.

14. Allison Young, "1 Timothy 2:11-15," *Christians for Biblical Equality International;* www.cbeinternational.org/?q=content/1-timothy-211-15 (accessed May 17, 2012).

15. Matt Slick, "1 Tim. 2:15, she, they, and salvation through Child Bearing," *Christian Apologetics and Research Ministry;* http://carm.org/1-tim-215-she-they-and-salvation-through-child-bearing (accessed June 7, 2012).

16. Grady, 58.

17. Welton, 136; Young, "1 Timothy 2:11-15"; *Blue Letter Bible,* s.v. "Authenteō" (Strong's Greek#831);www.blueletterbible.org/lang/lexicon/lexicon.cfm?Strongs=G831&t=KJV (accessed May 18, 2012).

18. Maureen D. Eha, "She Will Not Remain Silent," *Charisma Magazine* (May 31, 2002); www.charismamag.com/index.php/component/content/article/260-cover-story/5988-she-will-not-remain-silent (accessed June 7, 2012). Also see Tami Reed Ledbetter, "'60 Minutes' segment on Anne Graham Lotz muddied SBC stance on women in ministry," *Baptist Press* (June 7, 2001); www.bpnews.net/bpnews.asp?id=11051 (accessed June 29).

CHAPTER 5: THE HEAD AND THE HELPER

1. Richard and Danielle Schmidt, "An Emancipation Proclamation: A Biblical Approach to the Role of Women in Leadership" (unpublished paper); "The Athanasian Creed," *Creeds of Christendom, with a History and Critical Notes, Volume 1: The History of Creeds;* www.ccel.org/ccel/schaff/creeds1.iv.v.html (accessed May 22, 2012). Matt Slick, "What is Arianism?" *Christian Apologetics and Research Ministry;* http://carm.org/arianism (accessed May 22, 2012).

2. Gilbert Bilezikian, *Beyond Sex Roles* (Grand Rapids, MI: Baker, 1986), 137-139.

3. Paul's discussion of covering the head in First Corinthians 11:3-16 is complex, and a full discussion of it is beyond the purpose of this book. For more on this passage, see *Discovering Biblical Equality,* edited by Pierce and Groothius, and *Beyond Sex Roles* by Bilezikian.

4. Gordon D. Fee, "Praying and Prophesying in the Assemblies," *Discovering Biblical Equal-*

ity, Ronald E. Pierce and Rebecca Merrill Groothuis, eds. (Downers Grove, IL: InterVarsity Press Academic, 2005), 149.

5. I. Howard Marshall, "Mutual Love and Submission in Marriage," *Discovering Biblical Equality,* Ronald E. Pierce and Rebecca Merrill Groothuis, eds. (Downers Grove, IL: InterVarsity Press Academic, 2005), 187-190

6. Bilezikian, 165-166.

7. For a further explanation of the yellow truck-red truck metaphor, see my book *Loving Our Kids on Purpose* (Shippensburg, PA: Destiny Image, 2008), 54-56.

8. *Blue Letter Bible,* s.v. "hypotasso" (Strong's Greek #5293) http://www.blueletterbible.org/lang/lexicon/lexicon.cfm?Strongs=G5293&t=KJV (Accessed September 19, 2012).

9. NASB notes for Genesis 2:18; www.biblegateway.com/passage/?search=gen%20 2:18&version=NASB (accessed May 23, 2012).

10. *Blue Letter Bible,* s.v. "Ezer" (Strong's Hebrew #5828); www.blueletterbible.org/lang/lexicon/lexicon.cfm?Strongs=H5828&t=NASB (accessed May 23, 2012).

11. *Blue Letter Bible,* s.v. "Azar" (Strong's Hebrew #5826); www.blueletterbible.org/lang/lexicon/lexicon.cfm?Strongs=H5826&t=NASB (accessed May 23, 2012).

12. Dee Dee Myers, *Why Women Should Rule the World* (New York: Harper, 2008), 107-110.

CHAPTER 6: THE GIFTS OF WOMEN

1. For more on this, see my book *Culture of Honor* (Shippensburg, PA: Destiny Image, 2009).

2. Malcolm Gladwell, *Blink* (New York, NY: Hachette Book Group, 2005), 249.

3. Gladwell, 250.

4. Gladwell, 248-9.

5. Gladwell, 247-8.

6. I heard this analogy from Theresa Dedmon, a friend of mine who models what it looks like to be a powerful woman.

7. Alica H. Eagly and Linda L. Carli, "The female leadership advantage: An evaluation of the evidence," *Pergamon: The Leadership Quarterly* 14 (2003) 807-834; www.wellesley.edu/Psychology/Psych/Faculty/Carli/FemaleLeadershipAdvantage.pdf (accessed June 8, 2012).

8. Dan Goleman, "The Brain and Emotional Intelligence," *Psychology Today* (April 29, 2011); www.psychologytoday.com/blog/the-brain-and-emotional-intelligence/201104/are-women-more-emotionally-intelligent-men (accessed May 28, 2012).

9. Eagly and Carli, 813-818.

10. Rita Webster, "Women and Leadership: Five Key Strengths Every Organization

Needs," *HR Management;* www.hrmreport.com/article/Women-and-Leadership-Five-Key-Strengths-Every-Organization-Needs/ (accessed June 8, 2012).

11. Richard Gray, "Scientists prove that women are better at multitasking than men," *The Telegraph* (July 17, 2010); www.telegraph.co.uk/science/science-news/7896385/Scientists-prove-that-women-are-better-at-multitasking-than-men.html (accessed May 28, 2012).

12. Jack Zenger and Joseph Folkman, "Are Women Better Leaders Than Men," *HBR Blog Network: Harvard Business Review* (March 15, 2012); http://blogs.hbr.org/cs/2012/03/a_study_in_leadership_women_do.html (accessed June 8, 2012). To read the full study, "A Leadership Study: Women do it Better than Men," see www.zfco.com/media/articles/ZFCo.WP.WomenBetterThanMen.033012.pdf (accessed June 8, 2012).

13. Dan Abrams, *Man Down* (New York: Abrams Image, 2011).

14. Shelley E. Taylor, Laura Cousino Klein, et al, "Behavioral Responses to Stress in Females: Tend-and-Befriend, Not Fight-or-Flight," *Psychological Review,* Vol. 107, No. 3, 411-429 (http://taylorlab.psych.ucla.edu/2000_Biobehavioral%20responses%20to%20stress%20in%20females_tend-and-befriend.pdf, Accessed September 19, 2012).

15. Dee Dee Myers, *Why Women Should Rule the World* (New York: Harper, 2008), 86-87.

CHAPTER 8: PERMISSION TO BE POWERFUL

1. *Blue Letter Bible,* s.v. "Maria" (Strong's Hebrew #3137); www.blueletterbible.org/lang/lexicon/lexicon.cfm?Strongs=G3137&t=KJV

2. Jimmy Carter, "Losing my religion for equality," *The Age* (July 15, 2009); www.theage.com.au/opinion/losing-my-religion-for-equality-20090714-dk0v.html?page=-1 (accessed June 5, 2012).

3. All information on Abraham Lincoln and Franklin Douglass was taken from Doris Kerns Goodwin, *Team of Rivals: The Political Genius of Abraham Lincoln* (New York: Simon & Shuster, 2006), 205-207, 406-407, 497, 551-553, 649-651.

4. Ibid., 207.

5. For more on this, see Ellen Weinreb, "How Job Sharing May Be the Secret to Work-Life Balance," *Forbes.com* (October 24, 2011); http://www.forbes.com/sites/work-in-progress/2011/10/24/how-job-sharing-may-be-the-secret-to-work-life-balance/ (accessed June 14, 2012).

6. For more on this, read my book *Culture of Honor* (Shippensburg, PA: Destiny Image, 2009).

List for suggested reading and listening

Books:

An Apple for the Road - Pam Spinosi and contributing authors

Beautiful One - Beni Johnson and contributing authors

Born to Create - Theresa Dedmon

The Chicken Coop Kid - Sheri Silk

Shorts in the Snow - Sheri Silk

One of those days - Sheri Silk

The Supernatural Power of Forgiveness - Kris and Jason Vallotton

Living from the unseen: Reflections from a transformed life - Wendy Backlund

What if... - Coming soon featuring Bethel authors, Sheri Silk, Beni Johnson, Dawna De Silva, Brittney Serpell and others!

Teaching CD's:

Shifting Atmospheres - Dawna De Silva

Women set free - Faith Blatchford

To be Known - Sheri Silk

Worship:

Still Believe - Kim Walker-Smith

For the Sake of the World - Jenn Johnson and Bethel Music

The Loft Sessions - Bethel Live CD

red arrow

Red Arrow Media is a company of media professionals with diverse, cosmopolitan backgrounds and a wealth of experience, all united by our desire to create, produce, and distribute excellent literary texts and other media worldwide. We offer a comprehensive menu of publishing services and specialize in helping both budding and seasoned authors find their literary voice, write and edit their texts, and create powerful and pleasing interior and exterior designs. We also connect our authors with a plethora of other media services, from printing and distribution to bookselling, website development, publicity campaigns, photography, and video production.

www.redarrowmedia.com